KITTY'S

STORY

FROM FERAL KITTEN

TO

REIGNING HOUSE CAT

LINDA BRENDLE

KITTY'S STORY
FROM FERAL KITTEN TO REIGNING HOUSE CAT

ISBN: 978-1-7342108-0-4
Ebook available

DEDICATION

To all the strays, whether on four legs or two,
who need food, shelter, and love.

*I will search for the lost and bring back the strays.
I will bind up the injured and strengthen the weak.*
Ezekiel 34:16

To Nancy —
Thank you for stopping
by. Enjoy!
Blessings,
Linda Brenelle

CONTENTS

	Preface	7
1	Taking in Strays – 6/14/15	9
2	Yes, We're Hooked – 6/21/15	11
3	Kitty Drama – 7/12/15	15
4	Letting Go – 7/26/15	17
5	Kitty in the Garden – 9/13/15	21
6	Who Owns Whom? – 9/30/15	23
7	Free Kittens Aren't Free – 11/22/15	25
8	Kitty Comes in from the Cold – 1/10/16	27
9	Kitty Has High Hopes – 1/31/16	29
10	Spike's Out of the Dog House, Kitty's in – 2/21/16	31
11	Kitty in Charge – 3/13/16	35
12	Nursing is not Kitty's Calling – 3/20/16	37
13	Kitty Trauma – 4/3/16	39
14	Angel Kitty or Cat from Hell – 4/24/16	43
15	Kitty Condo, Poke Salad, and Blackberries – 5/1/16	47
16	Socializing Kitty – 5/15/16	51
17	Happy Birthday, Kitty – 6/5/16	53
18	Country Life is not All Peace and Quiet – 6/12/16	55
19	Freedom's Limits –7/4/16	59
20	From Feral Kitten to Reigning House Cat – 7/17/16	61
21	Kitty Troubles – 8/14/16	63
22	Kitty, the Fickle Feline – 9/18/16	65
23	Cat TV - 10/2/16	67
24	People Food – 11/6/16	69
25	Kitty's New Year's Resolution – 1/8/17	71

26	How Old is Kitty – 3/19/17	75
27	Kitty: When She's Good – 4/9/17	77
28	Kitty: Interior Designer – 4/23/17	81
29	Anywhere She Wants – 5/28/17	83
30	Kitty Loves Us – 8/20/17	85
31	Kitty Missed Us – 9/17/17	89
32	National Cat Day – 10/29/17	91
33	Kitty Dislikes Changes, Too – 12/10/17	95
34	The Princess and the Kitty Bed – 1/7/18	97
35	Kitty's New Game – 3/18/18	99
36	Kitty's Tolerance is Growing – 4/29/18	101
37	A Tale of Kitty's Tail – 7/29/18	103
38	Kitty's Camping Experience – 8/12/18	105
39	Kitty, Where Are You? – 11/4/18	107
40	Kitty Unchained – 11/11/18	109
41	Kitty's Second Christmas – 12/2/18	113
42	Kitty and the Blanket War – 1/13/19	115
43	Kitty's Back! – 2/10/19	117
44	The Good Light – 3/10/19	119
45	Kitty Keeps Us Straight – 3/17/19	121
46	Pets and Their Rituals – 6/2/19	125
47	Kitty Meets a Fan – 7/28/19	129
48	Kitty Welcomes Us Home – 8/25/19	133
	A Note from Kitty	135
	About the Author	137
	More Books by Linda Brendle	139

PREFACE

Four years ago, a four-ounce black and white fur ball walked into our lives, and nothing has been the same since. At first, this tiny feral kitten was little more than a cute and amusing distraction from our outdoor chores. But as she demanded to be fed and petted, she soon became more.

She was an unending source of writing material for the City Girl column I write for the Rains County Leader, our local weekly newspaper. She soon became my most popular topic, and people who didn't remember my name knew I was the cat lady.

Then, she moved into the house of the two people who were adamantly opposed to having an indoor cat. Now she reigns over the Brendle household, and we are more than happy to be owned and ruled by our feline monarch.

Many of Kitty's fans asked if I planned to write a book about her. It wasn't on my original to do list, but after two memoirs about Alzheimer's caregiving and two novels about child trafficking, I decided something lighter was in order. I spent several weeks assembling and editing my columns about her into a viable manuscript. This book is about the little fur ball who grew into the beautiful, thirteen-pound semi-longhair tuxedo cat pictured on the cover. This is Kitty's Story. Enjoy!

Chapter 1

Taking In Strays – 6/14/15

June is Adopt-a-Cat Month – so we did. Truthfully, I'm not sure who adopted whom, but I'm getting ahead of my story.

Last week David and I were working in the back yard when I heard a noise I didn't recognize. My country education has progressed to the point that I can identify the barking of a squirrel and the cry of a hawk, but this sound was a new one.

"David, is that a bird of some kind, or is there a cat around here somewhere?"

Before he had a chance to respond, we heard the sound of rustling leaves near the porch, and out strolled a kitten, meowing at the top of its little lungs. That tiny package had quite a set of pipes.

A quick inspection told me she was a girl, at least I think so. I understand it's a little hard to tell with kittens, but we'll assume I'm right for now. She wasn't much more than a ball of black fur with four little legs tipped with white socks, a white belly, and a little white patch on one side of her nose.

She was as cute as any of the feline pictures on Facebook, but David and I agreed we didn't want a house cat. Still, she was mostly skin and bones, so I went inside to see what I could find to feed her. Unfortunately, the Wheat Belly Diet doesn't offer much in the way of cat food, and she didn't seem too fond of coconut milk.

The next day she was still hanging around, so I brought home some regular milk. She showed a little more interest in that, but she was so little she didn't seem to know how to lap it up. However, after I held her with her mouth touching the surface of it, she began to get the hang of it and managed a couple of swallows.

The third day my neighbor brought over a small baggy with some dry cat food. I put a little bit in a plastic lid with some warm water and offered it to Kitty. She went crazy, trembling all over while she licked the thin gravy off the crunchy bits.

Since then, her eating has improved, and she's become quite adventurous. She followed David to the compost pile, and she trotted over to the garden to meet the neighbor who was walking his two dogs. The dogs didn't take to the newcomer, so I scooped her up before they had her for lunch.

When the showers came Sunday afternoon, she stayed under the shelter of the porch steps for a while, then she went for a walk in the rain. She was beginning to fill out a little bit, but with her wet fur clinging to her body, she looked even smaller than normal.

When the rain stopped, I went outside with a small towel and gave her a rubdown. Then, David turned an empty plastic trash can on its side to provide a little more shelter from future downpours. All the excitement whetted her appetite, and she really chowed down on her dinner.

Several people have asked if we've named her. So far, we're just calling her Kitty – I think we're still in denial about having adopted a cat. There are six steps up to our porch, and Kitty has figured out how to climb as far as the second step. It won't be long before she finds her way up to the porch. Then, we'll see how long our resolve not to have a house cat lasts.

Chapter 2

Yes, We're Hooked — 6/21/15

Last week I wrote about the kitten we had adopted a few days before, or more accurately, the kitten who had adopted us. I ended by saying she had managed to climb the first two of six steps to our back porch, and I wondered how long it would take her to make it all the way up and, from there, into the house. It didn't take long.

I wrote the column on Sunday evening, and on Tuesday morning she said good morning at the top of the stairs. Then the rain came, and Wednesday morning it was coming down so hard that the plastic lids that serve as food and milk bowls would have been washed clean before she could swallow a mouthful. So, David brought her into the laundry room, and I served her breakfast inside.

Once she was happily chomping away, I closed her in and went to the kitchen to fix our breakfast. Before the food was on the table, I felt little furry paws on my bare feet, and there she was. When the builders installed the doors in our home, they used the same length door in all the doorways, regardless of whether the room was carpeted or tiled. Consequently, there is a Kitty-sized gap under the door between the kitchen and laundry room, and she took that as an open invitation. David showed her the error of her ways by blocking the gap with a towel and a couple of pairs of work boots.

After the rain let up, David went to the shed and found a large piece of plywood which he used to shield the opening of her trash can home from splashing rain. So far, she hasn't been back inside, but she has been traveling with us quite a bit this week.

Apparently, we aren't the only people who have been enticed by a winsome stray lately. Some friends from church were chosen in February by a Great Pyrenees puppy who has since become a beloved member of the family. He is so loved, in fact, that they couldn't bear to kennel him when they went away for a week, and they asked if we would house and dog sit while they were gone. When the request was made, we were happy to help them out. Then, Kitty appeared and the logistics became complicated.

We planned to stop by our house each day to pick up the mail and check on the garden, but Kitty still eats several times a day. If we left enough food to last from one visit to the next, it would draw ants and possibly predators. The house where we were staying was definitely not a place for a kitten, but leaving her outside was not an option. Even if Spike, the pet-in-residence, didn't think she was a snack, he might accidentally step on her. Finally, we decided to bring her with us, let her sleep in the garage at night, and then take her back to our place and let her play in the yard while I performed my part-time duties at the church.

Once the decision was made, we borrowed a pet carrier and made a quick trip to the store for a litter box, a bag of litter, and a bag of kitten food. She had enjoyed the cat food our neighbor brought for her to try, but David's Internet research said she needed something with more nutrition during her first year. Our free cat was getting expensive.

Her first trip in the car went well, if a bit noisily. She meowed and whined the whole time, and when David lifted the carrier out of the car, she was clinging to the mesh door like one of those Garfield dolls with suction cups on its feet. When the door swung open, Kitty swung right along with it. She's very adaptive, though, and since then, the twice-a-day trips have been quiet.

She has adjusted to the new environment and routine as easily as she adjusted to life at the Brendles. After one "oops" on a doormat, she has trained herself to use the litter box faithfully. She has also trained us to visit her frequently to make sure she isn't hungry, thirsty, or lonely. Over the weekend, we had a couple of cloudy days with a nice breeze, so we brought her out to the front porch with us where she played around our feet and stalked the legs of the table before going back to the garage to nap in her carrier.

As predicted by many of you, Kitty has quickly found a place in our family. I don't think she'll find a place in our bed any time soon, but who knows what will happen before my next column.

Chapter 3

Kitty Drama – 7/12/15

My columns have been relatively serious the last two weeks, but several people have asked me about Kitty, so it's time for an update. Besides, she has provided some very good writing material.

First things first – her name is officially Kitty. We took her to the vet for her first shots, and when the receptionist asked for her name, David and I hesitated. "Shall I just put 'Stray Cat'?" she asked. We couldn't have that, so we quickly agreed that Kitty would work for all of us.

The patient was fairly well behaved on the examining table, especially after the nurse gave her a wadded up piece of paper to bat around. She didn't appreciate some of the invasive tests and the shot, but she recovered her good nature quickly enough. She weighed in at 1.4 pounds, but the vet pronounced her healthy. The way she has been eating, I expect her weight to double by the time we take her back for a rabies shot this week.

She is still an outside cat, but we visit her frequently. She entertains us by racing up and down the steps, hopping after grasshoppers and crickets, and fighting with any stray twig or dry leaf that crosses her path. Sometimes, she stops long enough to allow us to scratch her ears, but she only stays for a few seconds before dashing off to battle some imaginary enemy. At one point, David wondered if she might need a scratching post, but she has discovered the bark of a tree will do nicely. She has also discovered her climbing skills, and frequently scrambles up a foot or two before jumping back down.

The first time I watched her climb, I had a feeling her adventuresome spirit might lead to trouble. She proved me right, and rather quickly. Last week, David went out one morning to feed her. She didn't come when he called, so he looked under the motor home and the car, her latest hangouts. She wasn't there, but he could hear her meowing. Finally, he looked up, and there she was, forty feet up in a tree with no idea how to get down.

I noticed him looking for her and stepped out on the porch to see if I could help. He pointed up, and I saw her huddled in the fork of two small limbs, wailing almost as pitifully as the first day she wandered out from under the steps. I grabbed a laundry basket, David lined it with an old rug from the shed, and we stood under the tree, trying to coax her down. She would move a few inches one way or the other, and then scoot back to where she felt safe. Finally, she walked out on a small branch that extended toward the house.

"I think she's over the roof," David said. "I'm going to get the ladder and climb up there. Maybe she'll jump to me."

I strained to see her among the leaves and tried to hold the basket directly under her. I heard rustling, and suddenly, I saw two little white-tipped feet suspended in mid-air.

"Hurry!" I yelled. "I think she's losing her grip."

Before the words were out of my mouth, a little black and white fur ball streaked down directly into the center of the waiting basket. Two huge eyes peeked up over the edge, and I heard her purring like crazy. If she could have spoken, I think she would have said, "Wow! Let's do that again!"

Later that day, since the ladder was already out, David used it to complete the installation of a window unit in our bedroom. He decided to leave the ladder out, just in case he needed to do some additional caulking, and it was still there on Sunday. After church, he took Kitty some milk while I prepared lunch. He found her sitting on top of the ladder, singing her plaintive song. As he walked toward her, she tried to come down on her own, and she tumbled all the way to the bottom. This time, there was no basket waiting to catch her.

Kitty has experienced some other traumas, like a bath to hopefully remove some of the fleas that find her particularly tasty, and an unexpected encounter with the septic system sprinklers, but none have been as dramatic as her climbing incidents. She doesn't seem to have suffered any permanent damage, but if I'm counting correctly, she's down to seven lives.

Chapter 4

Letting Go — 7/26/15

Kitty made her third and highest trip into the black gum tree outside our dining room window this week. When I went out to feed her Sunday morning, I heard her faint meowing, but I couldn't see her, hidden as she was in the thick leaves.

I interrupted David's shower with the news. "Kitty is in distress, and I can't find her."

By the time he made it outside, I had located our little adventurer, and we spent the next hour or so craning our necks and giving her advice as if we expected her to understand what we were saying.

"Kitty, just back down the tree the same way you went up."

"Come on! Jump down, and we'll catch you."

She wasn't having any of it, though. She was nestled into a crook next to the tree trunk where she felt secure, and she wasn't inclined to venture far from her nest.

David didn't quite trust her aim or our ability to position the laundry basket to catch her if she fell, so he had brought an old blanket from the shed to use as a kind of fireman's net. He also brought out folding chairs, I brought out coffee, and we sat in the shade, listening to Kitty's pitiful cries and discussing our options.

During the quiet moments, I began thinking like a writer and wondering what life applications I could draw from the situation. I thought of the verse in Psalm 91 that says, if you trust in God, His angels will "bear you up lest you strike your foot against a stone." I wondered if that applied to silly kittens in trees. I also thought about the many times I have found myself in a tight spot, frozen in place, afraid to let go and take a leap of faith.

When I realized we were going to be late for Sunday school, we decided I would go on to church while David stayed on Kitty watch. Everyone asked where he was, and I'm sure he will take a lot of kidding about his role as Feline Protector. Still, when he takes on the responsibility for someone, regardless of how small, he takes his commitment seriously.

I found it a little hard to concentrate on the service as I wondered what was going on at home. I breathed a few extra prayers for safety, hoping David wouldn't decide to climb up after her and end up in a mixed pile of husband and Kitty parts at the bottom of the tree.

My prayers were answered, but the situation had not changed much when I arrived back home. Kitty's wails sounded a bit more desperate, and David was standing under the tree rather than sitting in the shade, but other than that, neither of them was bent or broken – yet. Kitty was getting restless, though, and she had managed to work her way down a few feet, sometimes by stepping on a lower branch and sometimes by falling and grabbing.

For the next few minutes, we circled the tree as she continued to climb and slip closer to the ground. Finally, when she was about level with the roof, she began making her way along a branch toward the house.

"I'm going up on the roof," said David. "I think I can get her to jump to me." I was almost sure I had heard that before.

I continued my intermittent prayers while trying to maintain my position under the tree with the blanket draped over my outstretched arms. She was visible enough that I was pretty sure I could break her fall if she should come down; I wasn't as confident about my ability to catch David.

He made it up the ladder and onto the roof with no problem. He began calling her name, and Kitty began inching toward him. She was over the roof, but she was still reluctant to let go of the branch. David patiently continued to call her, and when she was close enough, he reached out and pried her little paws away from the limb.

She was fine as soon as her feet hit the ground. She drank a little milk and purred as we expressed our relief by scratching her ears and dangling sticks for her to play with. I continued to muse about the experience, and I thought about stories in the Bible when God called and people were reluctant to let go. Moses was reluctant to let go of his simple life as a shepherd when God called him to go back to Egypt; Peter couldn't let go of his fear when Jesus called him to walk on the water; and the rich young ruler was certainly reluctant to let go of his wealth to follow an itinerant preacher. In my own life, I've often been reluctant to let go of the status quo, even when the call is to something better. Hopefully, the next time I'm called to "let go and let God," He won't have to pry my fingers off the branches.

Chapter 5

Kitty in the Garden — 9/13/15

For those who have asked recently, Kitty is doing fine. She is still in residence at the Brendle home and is still an outside cat except on days when it's extremely hot or rainy. On those days she's invited into the laundry room where she enjoys lazing on the cool tile floor, playing with the work boots and shoes lined up in front of the washer and dryer, and occasionally turning over the trash can.

She continues to grow, weighing in last week at a whopping six pounds. She has also improved her tree climbing skills. A few weeks ago, David found her caught on a limb about twelve feet from the ground. I talked to her to keep her calm, while he brought the ladder around and climbed up to rescue her. Later that same day, though, she was following him around the yard like the puppy dog she sometimes thinks she is. When he stopped to check the mail, she dashed up a tree beside him and stopped at his eye level, giving him a see-what-I-can-do look.

"Don't do that, Kitty," he said gently.

She sighed and backed down the tree as if she knew what she was doing. Since then, we've seen her playing on the lower trunks of several trees, and she even appeared from among the foliage of one after we had spent several minutes calling her, but we haven't had any more distress calls.

Kitty has also discovered the garden. The first time she followed me out among the corn plants, she jumped and ran every time the wind blew a leaf against her back, but she soon learned what a fun place a garden can be. Those waving leaves were perfect toys for a kitten to bat around, and there was an endless supply of bugs to stalk.

She has a serious side, though, and she likes to help when she can. When I water, she supervises the placement of the hose, and she lies at the edge of the spray pattern to be sure the coverage is adequate. She's always on hand when it's time to harvest, especially when I'm picking purple hull peas. She

21

loves to hide under the plants and grab my hand when I reach for a pod, thus ensuring that I'm not lonely and that my heart is pumping at a suitably aerobic rate.

Last Saturday I decided to try some fall peas and beans – again. I planted some last year, and just when they were ready to bloom, the earliest frost in recent memory wiped them out. I planted earlier this year, and the dry heat burned them up as soon as they peeked out of the dirt. I don't know if they'll do any better this time around, but the rows were already prepared, and it's good exercise.

I had almost finished the first of three rows when Kitty joined me. I had loosened the soil, poked holes with the hoe handle, and dropped a couple of butter beans into each hole. I planned to finish the other two rows, then go back and cover all the seeds at one time. As I squatted to pull a few stray weeds, Kitty appeared to say good morning and see how I was doing. She allowed me to pet her for a few minutes before she disappeared, and I went back to the weeds. A few minutes later, I straightened up and saw her busily scratching away in the first row.

"Kitty," I said, "what are you doing?"

She looked up and said *Who, me* in kittenese, and took off for parts unknown. Further investigation revealed that she apparently likes butter beans as much as David, although for a different reason. She had disinterred half a dozen of the fat, white beans and had a great time batting them around in the loose dirt. I began replacing the stray beans, but she reappeared and fought me for her new toys as I tried to cover them up.

So, I frequently have Kitty in the garden. She's not much help – in fact, she's a bit of a nuisance – but she's good company, and she's a good subject of conversation and columns.

Chapter 6

Who Owns Whom? — 9/30/15

While I was raising my son, I often said that kids and pets will eventually make a liar out of you. For example, as soon as you tell the hostess he won't eat pot roast, he eats his and yours and asks for more. Later, when you tell Grandma he has learned his multiplication tables through the tens, he can't manage to count to three. And when you write a column bragging on Kitty's tree-climbing skills, your husband has to climb on the roof four days in a row to rescue her.

Two weeks ago I wrote that Kitty had learned to back her way down a tree and that we hadn't had any 911 calls from her in a while. The Monday after I submitted that column, we came home to find her whining pitifully from a perch fifteen feet in the air. After trying to talk her down, David climbed onto the roof and coaxed her out on a limb until he could grab her.

We had repeat performances Tuesday, Wednesday, and Thursday. I was losing patience with her, saying she was just doing it for attention. Then, Friday morning David saw a large feral cat who roams the neighborhood chasing her. He grabbed his BB gun, and although he was too slow to catch the intruder, he was able to stop Kitty before she was too far up the tree. She stayed grounded for a couple of days, but when we pulled into the driveway after church on Sunday, she didn't come to greet us like she usually does.

"She's up the tree again," I said with a sigh. I wasn't dressed for Kitty retrieval, so I went inside. David had pretty much perfected his rescue routine without my help, so after I put on my shorts and t-shirt, I headed to the kitchen to start lunch. David changed, too, checked the afternoon football schedule, and then went outside. In a couple of minutes, he stuck his head in the door.

"I thought you said she was in the tree."

"She was."

"Well, she's not now. She's on the front porch."

23

Since then, we've seen her climb up and down several times, so we're confident that David can stay off the roof for a while. That's not to say that she's not becoming quite spoiled. She's spent several nights in the house this past week. It was a medical necessity since we had her spayed on Wednesday. She wasn't allowed to have anything to eat or drink after midnight on Tuesday, so she spent the night in the laundry room in her carrier. After the surgery, we were told to restrict her activities for a few days, so she has continued to sleep indoors.

It's inconvenient to do the laundry while she's in there. First, there's hardly room to move without stepping on her since most of the floor space is occupied by her litter box and the sleeping pad we fashioned out of an old mattress pad. Second, it's hard to keep her out of the dryer, and finally, she hears me coming and waits at the door to dash out as soon as I open it a crack. It's easier to just let her roam the house rather than to fight her desire to explore. She's easy enough to capture, though. All I have to do is sit on the floor, and in a few minutes she comes to visit for a back rub or a wrestle.

We didn't intend to have a pet, but since Kitty walked out from under our steps a few months ago, we've become pretty attached. My cousin summed it up pretty well after reading one of my Facebook posts about her. "It's good to hear that you and David are adjusting well to being owned by a cat."

Chapter 7

Free Kittens Aren't Free — 11/22/15

Kitty has a couple of feline acquaintances who like to hang out at our place. One is a timid ginger cat who seems mostly interested in a free meal, but the other is an aggressive gray tom whose mission in life seems to be to make Kitty's life miserable. I think he may be the main reason she spends so much time in the trees.

One afternoon I looked out the window and saw both Kitty and the gray tormentor up in the branches, and he looked as if he was still pursuing her. I stepped out on the porch, and it startled him so much he fell out of the tree. He hadn't used up all his lives, though, because he hit the ground running and was gone in a flash. A few days later I saw a gray blur flash by the dining room window and realized he had chased Kitty under the RV. Like any protective father would do when his little girl is threatened, David grabbed his shotgun. Actually, it was his BB gun, but it didn't matter since the cat was gone before he had a chance to take aim.

While we were out of town last month, two of our neighbors tag-teamed to see that Kitty had fresh food and water each day, and both mentioned seeing the two visitors lurking around. Since we weren't in residence, they seemed to be more brazen about showing their faces, and there seemed to be a bit of a turf war going on. Two Saturdays ago, David heard the sounds of a cat fight, and I ran out to see if Kitty needed reinforcements. Her opponent had disappeared, but she was still in full fight or flight mode. Every hair on her body was standing on end, and when I accidentally brushed her tail, she growled and hissed and arched like a Halloween cat. I tried to coax her into the laundry room, but she wasn't trusting anybody, so I left her outside on her own.

Sunday afternoon was a different story. I went out on the porch to check her food and water, and she met me there. She was still a little skittish, but she looked from me to the door and back to me. Then, she sat down and said, "MEOW!" She doesn't say much, but when she does, she means it. I asked if she wanted to go inside, and she replied by rubbing against my leg. She spent the night in the laundry room.

We were house/cow/dog sitting the next week, so Monday we packed Kitty in the car along with other necessities for the next few days. When we arrived at Spike's house and let her out in the garage, she wouldn't put any weight on her back right foot. We put her back in her carrier and headed for the vet, and poor Spike couldn't figure out why we came and went without petting, feeding, or untethering him.

When we told the vet she had been in a fight two days before, he took one look at her leg and said she had been bitten, and the bite was abscessed. I'm not sure how he could tell since her fur was fluffed up again, but I had seen his degrees on the wall, so I took his word for it. He started talking about lancing and putting in a drain, but I was relieved when he said that would be his second choice. First he wanted to try an injection of antibiotic and another of anti-inflammatory. He must have had a gentle touch, because Kitty didn't complain when he gave her the shots, and by the end of the day, she was putting her foot down a little.

By the end of the week, she was back to normal, and when we returned home, she seemed ready for a romp outside. I haven't seen the other cats since we came back, but we've been feeding Kitty inside to hopefully cut down on the extra-family traffic. She's still not a real inside cat, but she has been spending most evenings in the laundry room. First, she's protected from both predators and the cold weather, and second, until someone comes up with health insurance for cats, we can't afford any more emergency runs to the vet.

Chapter 8

Kitty Comes in from the Cold – 1/10/16

Before I began my series on Advent back in December, I wrote about Kitty's encounter with a less than friendly neighborhood tom cat. She ended up with an abscessed bite on her leg and a rather larger veterinary bill. I also wrote that, once we returned home from house sitting with our dog friend Spike, she was well and ready for an outdoor romp. However, her attitude changed quickly.

She was okay physically, but as soon as she caught sight of her tormentor, she took shelter in the nearest tree. After that, she spent less time outside and more time in the laundry room. Then, it was time to wash clothes. It seemed cruel to make her go out, and it was a hassle to try and keep her from sneaking into the kitchen every time I opened the door – and that's how Kitty officially became an indoor cat.

The problem was that, having lived outdoors all her life, she lacked some of the manners of civilized society. She didn't understand that kitties are not allowed on the dining table and the kitchen counters, that curtains and venetian blind cords are not toys, and that the furniture is not an appropriate place for sharpening claws. We tried scolding and time outs in the dungeon – David's new name for the laundry room. Neither had much effect, so I sent an S.O.S. to my cousin, better known as The Cat Whisperer. She has trained her cat to walk on a leash among other amazing feats.

She gave me some tips and sent me links to some articles she thought might be helpful. I found some useful suggestions, but the bottom line is that a cat is going to do what she wants to do. The best a cat caregiver can hope for (apparently no one really owns a cat) is to encourage the cat to want to do what the caregiver wants it to do.

The first thing I learned was to replace punishment with aversion therapy. A well-placed squirt of water, or a lot of squirts, has discouraged Kitty from touring the food preparation and serving surfaces – most of the time anyway. Next I learned that, if I provide enough toys, maybe Kitty will leave the curtains and blind cords alone. We're still working on the scratching thing. We've provided a couple of alternatives to the couch arms, and have tried to make them appealing by treating them with cat nip. Unfortunately Kitty is among the fifty per cent of cats that are unaffected by the feline herb, and she's unimpressed by my demonstrations. We'll keep trying, though.

We don't trust Kitty's manners enough to leave her unsupervised in the house, so she still stays in the laundry room at night and when we're gone. She would prefer more of an open-door policy, but I've found a treat she likes, so she goes into her bedroom willingly enough. Kitty is still enough of a kitten that she prefers to wrestle and play fight rather than cuddle, but she's beginning to allow us to pet her a bit more, especially when she's first allowed out of her room. She also naps on my ottoman or at David's feet when he lies on the couch to watch TV.

All things considered, we're all pretty happy with the new living arrangements. It's been a long time since I've had cats instead of dogs, and it's taken a while to get adjusted to the differences. It helps when I remember the opposite attitudes of the two pets. Dogs think like this: "You feed me, you give me a warm place to sleep, you pet me – you must be God." On the other hand, a cat's attitude is: "You feed me, you give me a warm place to sleep, you pet me – I must be God."

Chapter 9

Kitty Has High Hopes – 1/31/16

In 1959 the song "High Hopes" became popular after Frank Sinatra sang it in the movie "Hole in the Head." With its lyrics about an ant who moved a rubber tree plant and a ram who butted a hole in a dam, the song became an anthem of encouragement for both anyone who was discouraged and anyone who had big ideas. Recently, there have been times when Kitty has reminded me of that song.

It's said that cats are extremely curious. That's especially true when a closed door is involved. Regardless of which side of the door they're on or how recently they've been on the other side, the grass is always greener, the carpet is softer, or there are more toys on the other side.

Kitty loves Saturdays because that's the only day when David and I might possibly stay home all day and she doesn't have to spend any time in the Dungeon, also known as the laundry room. She really likes it when the weather is nice, because the exterior doors are opened many times during the course of the day. When David goes out to cut and burn trees, till the garden, or mulch the dry leaves, Kitty runs out the door just ahead of him. A few minutes later when I take out the trash or make a trip to the compost pile, she runs back in. Then, when I come in, she goes back out again.

Interior doors are equally fascinating to her, at least when they're closed. Even though she is released from the Dungeon when we're home, she still doesn't have free run of the house. Since she isn't yet civilized enough to be trusted out of sight, the doors to all three bedrooms and both bathrooms stay closed. She is fully convinced that Kitty heaven lies behind those doors, and she spends a great deal of time trying to prove the accuracy of her theory.

She has discovered by experimenting with an occasional open door that she can swing one of the mysterious barriers back and forth by hooking her paw under it. She hasn't quite learned that the technique that works on an open door doesn't have the same effect on a closed one. When she and I are on opposite sides, I often see a white-tipped Kitty foot poking under the door. Her high hopes are cute until she turns her attention downward and tries to dig her way under by scratching at the carpet. That's when we have a talk about unacceptable behavior, sometimes reinforced with a spray bottle.

She's an observant little thing, though, and pretty smart for her age. She has noticed that there is something special about the shiny round things about halfway up the door. One morning last week I was blow-drying my hair when I caught a flash of movement in the bathroom mirror. That mirror gives me a view into the bedroom and across the bed to the opposite wall – which incidentally includes the closet door.

I turned off my dryer for a minute and put down my brush, curious about what I had seen. I didn't have to wait long. A second or two later I saw a ball of black fur bounce up from behind the bed, extend one white paw, and take a swat at the door knob. She bounced up a couple more times before my laughter broke her concentration, and she came into the bathroom to find out what was so funny. Since then, she has made several more assaults on door knobs, sometimes using two paws, one on either side. So far, she has been unsuccessful, but she still has high hopes.

Chapter 10

Spike's Out of the Dog House, Kitty's in – 2/21/16

I have a confession to make. Last week I wrote about Spike, the reigning canine of the ranch where we're house sitting for three weeks. He had been leaving me "gifts" on the floor of the barn where he spends the night, and I was not happy. Then, I discovered it was my fault.

Spike's food is kept in a tub in the garage with a one-pound coffee can for measuring his daily ration. I thought that ration was two cans full, but my memory failed me. He is accustomed to one can per day along with whatever gross tidbits he scrounges up in the field. At the moment there are a couple of what look like old cow bones in the yard. Anyway, he had no trouble eating the extra food I gave him; he just had trouble waiting until morning to get rid of it. Now I'm back on the correct feeding regime, and he is back on the good dog list, at least as far as his night-time barn behavior is concerned.

Kitty on the other hand has not been doing so well. As I've mentioned, she stays in the garage when we're house sitting with occasional supervised play time on the patio. The first sign of trouble came when David noticed dusty little paw prints all over the windshield. He really doesn't like it when neighborhood strays take a stroll across the car, but Kitty has to do something to entertain herself when left alone in the garage all night – so he forgave her. Then, she went too far. One night she apparently tried to leap directly from the floor to the roof. She must have fallen short and slid down the passenger door leaving four little vertical claw marks right through the red paint. Since then, we've been parking in the carport, and she is in the dog house, so to speak.

Meanwhile, Spike had been busy. Although I wouldn't say he's back in the dog house, we did have an interesting afternoon with him on Friday. We were getting ready to go to our weekly home group Bible study, so I was watching for an opportunity to tether him before we left. He had spent most of the afternoon snoozing on the patio, so I expected it to be an easy task. However, I didn't count on the manure truck.

Spike's people had ordered a load of natural fertilizer for the hay field just south of the house. I had just grabbed a doggy treat and was headed for the door when I heard a loud grinding noise coming from the field. Through the glass pane in the door, I saw Spike's ears perk up, and I knew I was in trouble. What looked like a long dump truck with a spreader of some sort on the front came into view, and it was slinging what looked like clumps of dark, rich Texas soil all over the place. By the time I reached the patio, Spike was happily rolling in the dark stuff, and I could tell by the smell that it wasn't soil.

I went back into the house and picked up his leash and began walking slowly toward him. He had, at this point, switched from rolling to nibbling. He sensed when I was getting too close and managed to keep just out of reach. I tried to watch where I stepped, but by the time I gave up and returned to the house, I had about half an inch of yuck on the bottom of my shoes. I changed shoes and told David I didn't think I could catch up with Spike before time to leave, so we would have to leave him loose.

The problem is that Spike is drawn to the sound of engines of any kind, and before the car was a hundred feet from the house, Spike was standing in front of us. David stopped, I got out of the car, and Spike ran away, snickering and saying *nanner, nanner, nanner* in doggy talk. We did that same dance a couple more times, but the saying is that you can only fool <u>some</u> of the people all of the time, so we finally moved on toward the gate.

Predictably, Spike followed us out the gate and down the road. My hope was that, when we reached the end of his property, he'd crawl under the fence and go back to the chicken poop. No such luck. He continued to follow us, and we clocked him at twenty-five miles an hour. When we reached the mile mark, his tongue was hanging out, and he was beginning to fall behind. We found a good spot to turn around and headed back to the house, hoping he'd follow. He did, and David took it easy on him, slowing down to fifteen.

When we were a short distance from the gate, Spike took a short-cut under the fence. He made a brief stop at the front pond for a quick dip and a drink, but he still beat us back to the house. He was getting another drink out of the rain barrel when I got out of the car, and after a brief game of "catch me if you can," he allowed me to take hold of his collar, lead him around to the patio, and hook him up for the evening.

Since then, he and Kitty have both been pretty good, but they have plenty time to think up more mischief. Spike's people will be gone for ten more days.

Chapter 11

Kitty in Charge — 3/13/16

Kitty has spent most of the week reestablishing her dominance of the Brendle household. Several weeks ago, while we were still house sitting, I mentioned that she was in the metaphorical dog house after using her claws on the passenger door of our Pontiac. Unfortunately, that wasn't the end of her mischief. One day when she was particularly bored, she amused herself by clawing the weather stripping on the doorway from the garage into the house and chewing on the corners of a small wooden bench. I later found out that the chewed corners were Spike's work, Spike being the resident canine, but she left enough of a mark to require drastic measures to prevent more damage.

After her lapse in good behavior, Kitty came into town with us when I went to my part-time job at the church or when we went to lunch at the Senior Center. We dropped her off at our house where she spent the day in the laundry room. Granted, The Dungeon isn't exactly spacious, but at least she had room to stretch her legs. As an added bonus, she could empty the shelves when she wasn't napping. We picked her up on our way back to The Ranch where she spent her unsupervised time in the garage in her pet carrier.

Other than the peace of mind of knowing she wasn't destroying someone else's house, this arrangement yielded another advantage for David and me. Kitty endured her incarceration without protest, and when we visited her, she was a completely different animal. When she was released from her carrier, instead of exhibiting her usual good-natured combativeness, she was docile and seemed to enjoy several minutes of petting. There were times when she even allowed me to draw her onto my lap, and sometimes she let me pick her up without protest.

All that changed as soon as we returned home. Once she was released into the house at large, it became Fast & Furious time as she raced from one end of the house to the other, again and again. She is a single cat who weighs ten to twelve pounds, but she sounds like a herd of buffalo stampeding across the carpet and tile. Once she slowed down a bit, she began to reacquaint herself with the toys we didn't take with us. She has fallen in love again with the stuffed fish with the feathered tail, carrying it around in her mouth with the pole trailing along behind. The one thing she has totally ignored is her scratching post, choosing instead to sharpen her claws on the carpet and the furniture.

The most disappointing part of her return into polite society is the reemergence of the teeth and claws. When I let her out of the laundry room in the morning, she still purrs and rubs against my ankles, but when I lean down to pet her, she allows only a stroke or two before she grabs my hand with her paw or nips at a finger or two. I know that she just wants to play, but it feels like she's sending me a message similar to one David saw on Facebook this week. A picture of a tiger had the following caption: *I really like it when you pet me, but I still kinda want to eat you.*

I understand from other friends who are owned by cats that this is par for the course. I can only hope that, with time and maturity, Kitty will mellow a bit, becoming more of Dr. Jekyll and less of Mr. Hyde.

Chapter 12

Nursing is not Kitty's Calling – 3/20/16

It's been several decades since I've shared my home with a cat, and I don't remember how they reacted when I was sick. However, I've owned several dogs, and most of them were very empathetic when I didn't feel well. I had a cocker spaniel who would lie down with me when I was in bed with a cold, and later, I had a malamute/husky mix who laid his head in my lap if he thought I was feeling down. Kitty is not nearly as concerned.

I felt a cold coming on Tuesday – that scratchy feeling in the back of my throat that let me know the next week or two wasn't going to be pleasant. By Wednesday night, I was feeling rough enough that I skipped AWANA, and Sunday I gave up and stayed in my pajamas all day. I woke up feeling like, for lack of a better phrase, something the cat dragged in. My head hurt, and I ached all over. My nose was stuffed up and running, all at the same time, my throat was sore, and I had a cough that sounded like the horn of an old Model T. To make matters worse, David was complaining of a sore throat.

After I texted a couple people to cover our respective responsibilities at church, I snuggled into my big cozy chair under an afghan, and settled in for a nap. Kitty had other ideas. The cat who normally won't sit in my lap was all over me. She chased every movement of my hands and arms, and when I convinced her to get down, she amused herself by rearranging the fringe of my afghan. She soon became bored with my lack of participation in her games, so she made a quick tour of the living room and kitchen, knocking the place mats off the table, a silver vase off the bookshelf, David's glass off the coffee table (thankfully it was empty), and the squirt bottle I use to try and convince her to do things my way off the end table by my chair.

I finally accepted the inevitable. I folded the afghan and picked up the trail she had left. Then, I made myself a cup of coffee and sat down to read. In the meantime, Kitty dusted off her paws and, since her work was done, she curled up on the dining room chair by the bay window and went to sleep.

She visited me several times throughout the day just to be sure I was awake, but she delivered the final insult in the evening. When I sat down with my computer to write my column, I looked over at the couch where David had spent the day nursing his sore throat. Kitty was curled up on his legs, sound asleep. At least she gave me something to write about.

Chapter 13

Kitty Trauma — 4/3/16

When Kitty was younger, at that age we all go through when we have more courage than sense, she learned to scale a tree quite a while before she figured out how to climb back down. She gave David and me some anxious moments, and she provided me with a column or two about David's adventures when he climbed a ladder and coaxed her from her tree-top perch to the relative safety of the rooftop, and from there, back down to the ground.

After some unpleasant encounters with neighborhood feline bullies, she has become much less courageous and is content to watch the world through the windows while she relaxes in the security of the great indoors. However, she recently discovered that sometimes being under the roof can be as scary as being on top of it.

Normally, Saturday is her favorite day, because that's the day David and I catch up on chores in the house and in the yard. The doors are opened frequently, and she can dash out for a quick look around or hurry back in when she feels the least bit threatened. This past Saturday started out quietly enough – and then the roofers showed up. David has owned this house since before we met, and after almost twenty years of Texas weather, it needed some new shingles.

Kitty became restless when she heard two unfamiliar trucks pull into the driveway accompanied by the voices of four strange men. Then, three of the four men climbed up on the roof with a couple of shovels and a pitchfork and began the very noisy process of removing the old shingles. There were heavy footsteps and accompanying work sounds that vibrated the walls and rattled the dining room chandelier and the exhaust fans in the kitchen and bathrooms. Kitty disappeared.

I knew she was safely inside, so I went about my chores, looking in her usual hiding places when I passed them but not really worried. At one point, I went into the laundry room to remove the sheets from the washer, and I heard scratching noises coming from behind the dryer. Two white paws appeared on the top edge of the appliance followed closely by a couple of flat ears and two huge eyes. Kitty scrambled up onto the top, looked accusingly at me and suspiciously at the offending ceiling, and ran under the bed.

We didn't see much of her for the rest of the day. She came out when the crew took a break for lunch and, during the quieter parts of the operation, she stalked back and forth through the house, indignant at the disruption of her weekend. As the day and the work wound down, she ventured over to one of her favorite perches on top of a box of ancient LPs. It gives her a view of the back yard so she can monitor the activities of the local wildlife. She stretched up, put her front paws on the window sill, looked out in the yard, and immediately jumped down and ran back into the bedroom. David looked out to see what and spooked her and saw one of the workers raking up debris. Have I mention that she's not very brave?

Finally, the job was done and peace was restored. Kitty spent an hour or so checking out all her favorite spots – the ottoman in front of my chair, my computer case, the back of the sofa, and the dining room chair by the bay window – and then she stretched out and took a nap. Replacing a roof is exhausting.

Before I bring this to a close, I have to tell a tale on myself. I've had roofs replaced on a couple of homes before this, but the work always happened while I was at work. I was curious about the process, so I went outside from time to time to watch and to talk with the supervisor. It was an educational experience, and I also received an object lesson in the collateral damage of curiosity.

After the shingles were removed, I heard the sound of some kind of machine. I saw what looked like sawdust falling off the eaves, so I went outside to see what was going on. As I stepped out onto the front porch, I was covered by a shower of dust, oak blossoms, twigs, and bits of shingle. The noise was a leaf blower one of the guys was using to clear the roof of debris before laying down the new felt and shingles. He apologized profusely, but I laughed and reassured him it was my fault. I backed away to a safe distance and watched for a while, dusting myself off the best I could before going back inside.

We now have a beautiful new roof, and peace has been restored to the Brendle household. Kitty still seems a little skittish, but hopefully she'll be fully recovered from her trauma and back to normal soon. As for me, I think I'll be more careful about stepping outside the next time I hear an unidentified noise.

Chapter 14

Angel Kitty or Cat from Hell — 4/24/16

A lot has changed in Kitty's life since the last time I devoted a complete column to her. Most of the changes began when David discovered a program on Animal Planet called "My Cat from Hell." I don't think he really believed Kitty was that bad, but he thought he might find some tips on how to restrain some of her more irritating habits, like scratching on the furniture and using our bare feet for toys.

The show features Jackson Galaxy, a cat behaviorist who visits the homes of people with pets that behave so badly they are in danger of being "re-homed." It's an entertaining way to spend some down time, so David and I watched the show together for several weeks until we began to see repeats. Then David switched channels, and I reviewed what we had learned.

First, we learned that, compared to some cats, Kitty is an angel. She uses her litter box, and any scratches or nips have been the result of over-zealous playing instead of nastiness. According to Jackson and other cat owners I've talked with, those incidents are probably our fault. When she was younger, before her teeth and claws could actually hurt, we played with her with our hands, which is a big no-no. I've been on the lookout for new toys, although balls of foil are still her favorite. I've also resorted to rubbing lemon juice on my feet and hands a time or two. That's supposed to be a turnoff for her, but so far it hasn't been much of a deterrent.

Next, we learned that cats need things and spaces they can "own." That can be as simple as a strategically placed cat bed or as elaborate as a series of cat trees, shelves, and tunnels. I decided to try something in between.

Kitty has a bed in the laundry room, and there's a dining room chair by a window where she spends a lot of time. There's also a window in the living room that she can see out of by standing on a box of old LPs and putting her paws on the sill.

Then, there's a couch, a couple of chairs, and several forbidden tables. Not much Kitty ownership there.

I surveyed the living room for a while and settled my attention on the companion window to the one above the records. This window was blocked by a wing-backed chair that no one ever sat in. The chair was flanked by a small built-in cabinet on one side and on the other side by a large speaker from another era that has been incorporated into our entertainment center. I pulled the chair away from the wall where it still sits, waiting to be re-homed. I shared my plans with my neighbor Connie, and she contributed a carpeted pedestal that is the same height as the window sill. I removed the knick knacks from both the cabinet and the speaker, and Kitty has spent many happy hours wandering from surface to surface or sitting at the open window, watching "cat TV."

She loved her new space, but she wanted more. She tried sitting on the sill over the records, but either she leaned out too hard or she was chasing a bug. Either way, the screen and the cat ended up on the ground outside. After that, she turned her attention to a window on the other side of the living room. It had been forbidden territory because, in order to reach it, she had to cross an end table. Still, the view that was hidden behind a slightly opened mini blind drew her. Finally, I gave in and raised the blind a foot or so. Now she's allowed to sit on the table as long as she doesn't mess with my stuff.

At first, the extra freedom seemed to agitate her. A couple of nights, she was into so much mischief that I put her into the laundry room early where the worst she could do was knock a few cans and spray bottles off a shelf. Then, Saturday night she mellowed out. Maybe it was because she spent half the day working in the yard and the garden with David and me, or maybe the magic of having her own space was setting in. At first, she was so calm that I was afraid she was sick, but by Sunday night I was beginning to really like the new Kitty.

She still won't sit in my lap, but she does let me pet her a little more often. Sunday night she tried to knock David's glass off the coffee table once just to see if he was paying attention. She also jumped on my feet as I walked by on my way back to my chair, but there were no teeth or claws involved. As I write, she's lying half on the dining room tile and half on the living room carpet, surveying her kingdom. For the moment, that's angelic enough for me.

Chapter 15

Kitty Condo, Poke Salad, and Blackberries — 5/1/16

The last couple of weeks have been a time of counting blessings at the Brendle house. Nothing really big, but like dynamite, blessings often come in small packages. I'd like to tell you about three of ours.

The first was poke salad. Until we moved to Emory, all I knew about poke salad was that it was the subject of an Elvis song from the late sixties. Then, two years ago, someone brought some poke salad to the Senior Center. David and I checked it out and realized we had lots of it growing around our back yard. I had heard a lot of stories about the dangers of the green, so I did some on-line research and harvested some. Both of us enjoyed it, and neither of us suffered any ill effects, so I added it to my list of menu items.

For some reason, I didn't pick any last year. However, someone brought some to the Center recently, and David looked wistfully at it, so that afternoon I visited our back yard patch. I filled one Walmart bag and part of the second, expecting it to cook down a lot. Not so much. Thankfully, we both like leftovers, because we had poke salad for three nights.

The next blessing came last week after I wrote about my plans to provide Kitty with some personal space by putting a carpeted pedestal in one of her favorite windows and clearing nearby surfaces. As usual, I received a few comments about the on-going adventure of being owned by a cat, and then on Wednesday, one of my friends at the Senior Center called me over.

"I read your column this week. This morning I was work-ing at Good Samaritans (our local thrift store that is only open to the public on Saturdays), and they have a cat tree that you really need to get for Kitty. It's one of those three level things."

It sounded interesting, and I told her I'd be at the Thrift Store at 8:00 am Saturday to take a look at it. Then, I found out that David had made an appointment to have some repair work done on the car at 8:00 am in Sulphur Springs. That might have been a problem except that our neighbors, Dirk and Pat, go to the "Saturday sale" every week. I asked if I could bum a ride, and they picked me up at 7:45.

When my friend had described the cat tree, I envisioned something with three carpeted platforms on three posts. I wasn't prepared for a homemade stair-stepped Kitty condo with three cubes on the bottom, two in the middle, and one on the top. There were round openings in the walls between the cubes, and all the edges and surfaces were carpeted. Some of the edges had been well used by little teeth and claws, but it was a steal at ten dollars.

Dirk graciously loaded it into the back of his truck, delivered it to my house, and helped me put it into place. Kitty spent the next thirty minutes sniffing every square inch of her new playhouse. Since then, she has spent many happy hours checking out the view from various cubes and roaming from level to level. The new may wear off eventually, but for right now, she's been even more of an angel than she was last week.

The third blessing was the blackberries. When we bought our property, there was already a small slab at the back where a previous owner had intended to build. So far, we haven't done anything with it except park our tow dolly on it – but in the Spring, it becomes a focal point, because there are blackberry vines on the north and west sides.

Saturday, after I had arranged Kitty's condo and David had returned from the car dealership, he suggested it was time to go berry picking. I agreed, so we donned our rubber boots and sloshed through the puddles from Friday night's rain. David loves blackberries, but all the bending hurt his back, so I don't think he had a very good time. I'm closer to the ground so I don't have to bend as much, but my legs did tire after a while. Still, I love the idea of going out in our own back yard and finding something good to eat, so I had a great time. We harvested enough for a cobbler, a jar of jam, and a few berries left over to share with Connie and Charles across the street. (The jam recipe was supposed to make three jars, but this was my first attempt, and I guess I left too much berry on the seeds when I ran them through the sieve.)

48

Grace is often described as the freely given, unmerited favor and love of God. I'll leave it to each reader to decide whether God really cares about Kitty condos, poke salad, or blackberries, but as for me, I'm grateful for every bit of grace and for each blessing, even the small ones.

When the Lord your God brings you into the land he swore...to give you – a land with large, flourishing cities you did not build, houses filled with good things you did not provide, wells you did not dig, and vineyards and olive groves you did not plant...be careful that you do not forget the Lord.
Deuteronomy 6:10-12

Chapter 16

Socializing Kitty – 5/15/16

Kitty has continued to be angelic – either that or we have lowered our expectations. It's probably a bit of both.

Since I bought her Kitty condo, she has spent many hours in it – staring out the window, sleeping, and finding loose threads to chew on. When she tires of that, she plays with the curtains or tries to climb the mini-blind that I have raised halfway up the window trying to get it out of her reach. We're thinking about removing both the curtain and the blind to avoid arguing with her. As I said, we've lowered our expectations.

I'm still expecting her to become more companionable someday. It frustrates me that she won't sit with me and let me pet her. Since I find everything else on the Internet, I did a search on how to encourage her to be more of a lap cat. One suggestion was to get a generous supply of treats and settle into a comfortable chair with a good book. The idea is to lure the reluctant cat to you by tossing her a treat occasionally. Then, you encourage her to come near by placing each treat a little closer. Eventually, when she is close enough, offer the treat in your hand, and finally, don't release it until she puts her paws in your lap. Supposedly, she will come to relate being close to you with something pleasant, and you will have your lap cat. The caution is that, depending on the timidity of your cat, the process may take as long as a year.

Kitty is moving along much more quickly than that. First of all, I don't have to lure her onto the chair. As soon as she hears me open the drawer where the treats are stored, she appears at my feet and follows me. When I sit down, she jumps into my lap and begins searching. She takes the treat from my hand, but instead of lying down for a visit, she jumps down and enjoys the tasty bit on the floor. Then she jumps back into my lap to see if there are any more. If so, we repeat the process. If not, she goes elsewhere.

She's still not a lap cat, but she allows us to pet her more often when she is standing either on the floor or on a perch of some sort. When she's feeling friendly, she will present herself by rubbing on a leg or sitting on the floor and staring at one of us. She actually jumped into our laps the other night when we were on the phone, face-timing with the grandkids. Jealousy may work better than treats.

She is becoming more sociable in her own way. In fact, she and David have developed a night-time game. After he turns off the TV, he likes to get into bed and read for a while before turning out the light. I'm usually not quite ready to retire when he does. I have to finish the chapter I'm writing or rinse the last few dishes that have magically appeared in the sink since dinner – and I have to put Kitty to bed. While she waits for me, she hops up onto the bed and the game begins.

David arranges his pillows against the headboard, settles back against them, and slides his feet under the cover. Then, she pounces, first on one foot and then the other, depending on which one is moving. David usually tires of the game before she does and turns his attention to his book. When that happens, she lies down between his feet, gathers all four of her own paws into a bundle, and fights with them.

That part of the game must be pretty boring, because before long, she hops down and goes exploring to see what else she can get into. That's my signal that it's night-night time for Kitty. I have learned one lesson in using treats for training pur-poses. I no longer offer them close to bedtime. After she's had one or two, it becomes much more difficult to use them to lure her into the laundry room where she sleeps. She will follow me halfway, then give me that "gotcha" look before walking away with her tail in the air.

I have her number, though. She may have me wrapped around her little paw, but I'm still somewhat smarter. I follow her to wherever she decides to perch, wave the treats under her little black and white nose, and go into the laundry room alone. I rattle her food dish, and by the time I put the treats down on her food mat, she's right beside me, rubbing against my leg. As aloof and finicky as she tries to be, her tummy always betrays her.

Chapter 17

Happy Birthday, Kitty – 6/5/16

At some point during the last few weeks, Kitty celebrated her first birthday. I really shouldn't say she celebrated since we didn't think about it until we stopped by the vet's office. We needed some Revolution to deal with the fleas she has been bringing into the house – at least the ones that stay on her. We'll have to bomb the house to deal with the rest of them. The first time we took her to see the vet, he estimated her age based on her weight. Last week their records showed her as one year and one month old. That would make her birthday May 7, give or take a week.

I wrote my first column about Kitty for the June 16 edition last year. It was interesting to go back and see how much has changed since then. Here are a few *then* and *now* comparisons:

Then: We heard the sound of rustling leaves near the porch, and out strolled a kitten, meowing at the top of its little lungs.

Now: Kitty is relatively soft spoken, confining her remarks to purrs, chirps, and an occasional quiet meow. She does, however, express her displeasure very effectively with a quick swipe of her paw or a flash of her teeth.

Then: She was mostly skin and bones...[not] much more than a ball of black fur with four little legs tipped with white socks, a white belly, and a little white patch on one side of her nose.

Now: She has filled out from a scrawny four to five ounces to a healthy ten pounds. Her thin, spiky fur has been replaced with a full, sleek coat that looks beautiful on her but not so much on the carpet.

Then: I brought home some regular milk. She showed a little more interest in that, but she was so little she didn't seem to know how to lap it up.

Now: She has obviously overcome any eating difficulties she had a year ago. She is a good eater and has developed none of the picky habits cats are famous for. A friend whose cat disappeared gave us some canned cat food, but she licked it a bit before pushing it out of the bowl and onto the floor and turning her attention to her IAMs kibble.

Then: David turned an empty plastic trash can on its side to provide a little more shelter from future downpours.

Now: She has a three-story carpeted Kitty condo and more toys than any one cat needs, and we have rearranged the living room furniture to meet her requirements.

Then: Since then...she's become quite adventurous. She followed David to the compost pile, and she trotted over to the garden to meet the neighbor who was walking his two dogs.

Now: She is still adventurous, but she stays close enough to the house to run for cover if she comes under attack by a roving feral cat. She has become quite the hunter, though. Several times recently she has come home with legs hanging out of her mouth. Once it was a salamander, but when she put it down on the porch to play with it, it slipped through a crack between the boards. Now she sticks to frogs.

Then: She was as cute as any of the feline pictures on Facebook, but David and I agreed we didn't want a house cat... So far, we're just calling her Kitty – I think we're still in denial about having adopted a cat. There are six steps up to our porch, and Kitty has figured out how to climb as far as the second step. It won't be long before she finds her way up to the porch. Then, we'll see how long our resolve not to have a house cat lasts.

Now: For any regular readers of my column, there is no question about how this worked out. She is now an official member of the Brendle household. She's not yet trusted with unlimited access when we're not home, but her privileges continue to expand. She has captured our hearts - and in answer to a question asked by my cousin, we don't mind at all being owned by a cat. Happy Birthday, Kitty.

Chapter 18

Country Life is not All Peace and Quiet — 6/12/16

One of the attractions of country life is the peace and quiet – being able to sit out in the yard and see only an occasional neighbor driving by or to sleep with the windows open on a cool spring night and smell the fresh air instead of pollution. Another thing I really enjoy on our little country homestead is the wildlife. We've sat at our dining table and watched the squirrels, rabbits, and all kinds of birds play and forage for food. One season an owl joined us for dinner every evening, and for two seasons, a pair of hawks were frequent visitors. Before we cleared the back part of the lot, we saw lots of deer grazing among the honey suckle and poison ivy, and even now a doe and her fawns will wander across occasionally. On special occasions, we've seen two foxes, an armadillo, a skunk, and more buzzards than people of our age need to see.

Looking out into our back yard is a little like looking at our own personal zoo. I'm not enough of a city girl, though, to think it's really as peaceful and quiet as it sometimes looks. I've seen enough animal shows on The Discovery Channel to know how the food chain works – and even though I prefer my chicken skinless, boneless, and wrapped in clear plastic, I know where it comes from. Still, I don't want to see it happen.

A few years ago, when our yard was still a deer hangout, a neighbor asked if he could set up a blind out close to the creek when bow season came around. I didn't even want to be involved in the discussion, so I deferred to David. David was raised in a hunting family, so he doesn't have the same emotional responses to the subject that I do. He told the guy he was welcome to hunt as long as he shared a little bit of the meat. The hunt was successful, but I was glad it happened when we were visiting with David's family in Louisiana – and I enjoyed the venison, but I was glad it arrived frozen and wrapped in plastic.

There have been other deaths around here, especially since Kitty has decided to become a hunter. I have to admit that I don't feel the same sympathy for her victims that I did for the deer, but frogs and lizards don't have the same cuteness factor. Even so, I'm still enough of a city girl that I don't like to come face to face with the reality, so I make David deal with the remains.

Something happened this past weekend, though, that brought me face to face with the life and death struggle that goes on around me every day. I was working in the garden and had stopped in the shade for a breather. The garden is very close to the lot next to ours. The lot is owned but unoccupied at the moment, and the weeds are tall enough to be baled. It was very quiet, and then I heard rustling about twenty yards away. Suddenly, a rabbit burst out of the weeds with a large fox in hot pursuit. The two raced past the storage shed out of sight and almost instantly reappeared only to disappear into the weeds. Another u-turn brought them back into sight, this time racing toward the shed which is set up on concrete blocks. I heard a metallic thud as if one or the other had hit either the wall or the wheel barrow that leans up against it. I assume it was the rabbit, and that it was stunned enough to allow the fox to catch up. I heard a soft squeal, and a moment later, the fox emerged on my side of the shed with the limp rabbit in its mouth.

The entire drama took less than five seconds, and I was stunned. I let out in involuntary cry of sympathy for the loser – I've always been a sucker for the underdog, especially if it's small and furry. The fox must have heard me. The victorious look on its face disappeared as it froze in place with its ears perked and its eyes wide. I don't know if it saw or smelled me, but either way, it took off to the other side of the yard, heading home with dinner. Another fox appeared from the weeds, but since it wasn't distracted by the chase, it saw me right away and ran toward the creek.

I've thought a lot about what happened since then. The event wasn't life shattering or even unusual, but it has led to a few changes around here:

- Foxes, while still beautiful animals, have switched from the cute and cuddly column to the possible predator column.
- There's one less bunny to steal produce from my garden.
- I'm not nearly as willing to let Kitty go out and play unsupervised.
- The frogs and lizards around here may be a little bit safer.

Chapter 19

Freedom's Limits — 7/4/16

After my ring-side seat at the fox versus rabbit race in which the rabbit came in second, I made some changes to the status of Kitty's independence. It turns out that I am as over-protective of Kitty as I was when I was raising my son. Since I don't think that rabbit lived to demand a rematch, and since I'm not sure if foxes discriminate between bunnies and kitties, I have greatly curtailed Kitty's outdoor freedom. In fact, I think she's been outside once in the last month, and I hovered over her the entire time.

On the other hand, her indoor freedom has taken a great leap forward. Several times in the last few weeks, we have left her loose in the house when we went out to work in the yard for a short time. David did walk in once to find her on the dining room table, but other than that small indiscretion, she seemed to be handling her new freedom well.

Then, one day last week, we left her free to roam when we went over to visit a neighbor for a few minutes. As often happens, the visit lasted longer than a few minutes, and suddenly it was time to go to the Senior Center. We went straight to the car and headed out. We were almost ready to come home before we remembered that Kitty was not in The Dungeon. We took a wait-and-see attitude, and what we saw was that she had probably slept through our entire absence.

One of my least favorite parts of our Sunday morning routine is convincing Kitty that she needs to go into the laundry room while we go to church. Based on recent performances, this last Sunday I decided to leave her loose again. When we came home, she met us at the door but immediately ran the other way. The only thing I found out of place was my computer case. I leave it on a TV table next to my TV watching/writing chair, and it's one of her favorite napping spots. I suspect that she was sleeping deeply, curled up on the case, when she heard David's key in the lock. The noise startled her, she jumped off the table, pushing off with her back feet and knocking the computer case to the floor. Regardless of how it happened, as long as that's the only thing I find out of place, she can continue to roam free – during the day anyway.

I'm not yet ready to give her free rein at night. She's way too energetic when our bedtime comes. In addition, we have a window unit in our bedroom, and we close the door to keep the cool air in. I'm afraid if she was left outside the bedroom, she would dig a hole in the carpet trying to get in, and if she was inside with us, she wouldn't have access to her litter box. Still, she has earned other freedoms, so who knows what the future holds. I just hope she doesn't follow the example of our founding fathers and stage an all out rebellion.

Chapter 20

From Feral Kitten to Reigning House Cat – 7/17/16

Yes, Kitty's transition is complete. A couple of weeks ago, due either to her excellent behavior or her uncanny ability to climb on forbidden surfaces without disturbing anything or leaving incriminating paw prints, Kitty earned her daytime freedom. However, she was still confined to the laundry room at night.

She enjoyed her new liberty, and her annoyance at her nighttime imprisonment became more obvious. When the laundry room was the standard, I was able to entice her with a few treats, and she was grateful for them. After she became a semi-free agent, I could hold a handful of tasty bits under her nose, and she would growl at me. Several nights I went to bed with a fresh scratch on my hand or arm from a flying claw or a disapproving tooth when I gave up coaxing and carried her to her bed. There had to be a better solution.

The problem was the bedroom door. We close it at night to keep the cool air from the window unit in the room, but that would also deny Kitty access to her litter box in the laundry room if we let her sleep with us. It was still two or three months before the temperatures would drop enough for us to leave the door open. I knew the solution was two litter boxes, but I didn't know where to put the second one. Then I noticed the tub in the master bedroom – the huge octagonal monstrosity that drains the water heater before the water level is ankle deep. Perfect.

We made a quick trip to the store and came home with not only a second litter box but also a cushy Kitty bed. That night we set up the litter box and a bowl of water in the unused tub and put her new bed on the quilt-covered cedar chest at the end of our bed. The first night, she was very concerned about the door that closed her out of the rest of the house. Then, when we turned out the lights, she spent some time racing around the floor and walking across our legs. Sometime around midnight, though, she settled down, and the three of us slept peacefully.

After the first couple of nights, she settled into the routine quite nicely. She has learned which surfaces are off limits and rarely wakes us up by knocking things onto the floor. Her bed is usually empty as she apparently prefers to sleep under ours, but maybe she'll warm up to it in time. Before we turn out the light for the night, she sometimes lies near our feet, but she no longer chases them every time we move. She has, however, developed an interesting way of waking me in the morning. At some point during the night, I apparently kick the cover off one leg, and around 6:00 am, give or take a few minutes, she begins licking my toes. If I don't respond in a timely manner, she nibbles. It's effective and less jarring than an alarm clock.

So here we are, a year later, with the feral kitten we swore would never be a house cat. To those of you who are now saying *I told you so*, you were right. Kitty rules!

Kitty Troubles — 8/14/16

Being a cat is not all kibble and naps. Kitty has had a difficult week. Her troubles started on Wednesday when David took her in for her annual shots.

We've taken her to the Emory Veterinary Clinic a couple of times, and we really like the people and the treatment she receives there. However, since Medicare doesn't cover cats, we needed a cheaper alternative. When the time came for Kitty to be spayed, we found the Animal Protection League in Sulphur Springs. It wasn't as convenient as the local clinic, but it was much less expensive, so that's where David took her for her shots.

The League gives vaccinations only from 10:00 am to 2:00 pm on Wednesdays, so when David and Kitty arrived, the waiting room was full – of dogs. Kitty was safe in her carrier, but she didn't care much for the ill-mannered canines who wandered around at the end of long leashes, barking, snarling, and even fighting among themselves while she waited patiently for over half an hour. When her name was finally called, she was taken to the back alone while David was told to stay in the waiting room. A few minutes later, Kitty was brought back out having received only one of three vaccinations she was scheduled for. David was told she was too stressed for them to give her the other shots. I've mentioned that Kitty doesn't like to be petted or picked up unless it's her idea. I suspect that "stress" was a euphemism for the displeasure she probably expressed with her teeth and claws.

To add insult to injury, she was weighed at the clinic, and she has grown to a healthy 12.8 pounds. I'm not sure how she has gained so much weight on two-thirds of a cup of dry food a day and a half dozen tiny treats each night, but the scales don't lie. I have tried to reassure her that a lot of it was probably water weight, but several times since then, I've found her parading in front of the mirror and meowing something that sounded vaguely like, "Does this fur make me look fat?"

In addition to her medical difficulties, she suffered a personal loss this week. One of the first toys I bought her after she began to spend some time inside was a stuffed cylinder about three inches long and an inch in diameter. It was covered with soft leopard print material and had a tail made of several feathers. It was attached by an elastic cord to an eighteen-inch wand. At first, she loved to chase it, grab it, and fight with it. She quickly chewed off the tail, but she still loved it. Lately, she didn't chase it as much, preferring instead to walk around with it in her mouth, dragging the wand behind her. Thursday, the day after her traumatic visit to the vet, the string broke. She carried the fish around for a while, and then she jumped up on my chair and dropped it in my lap. I'm not sure if the soulful look she gave me was a plea for me to fix it or bury it. I did neither, but she seems to have recovered quickly anyway. The tailless, wandless fish now lies, like many of her toys, abandoned in the middle of the living room floor.

Kitty's final indignity was a physical assault, and I have to confess that I was the perpetrator. I was doing laundry on Saturday, and I went into the closet to find some empty hangars. As usual, she thought it was a race, and she won. She sat, also as usual, right where I needed to work. I leaned across her to pick up a few hangars from the very organized pile on the floor. Then, I dropped a couple, and the noise startled her, making her dart out the door. She took only a couple of steps forward, though, before jerking back a little. Then, she took off like a shot, and I didn't see her for a while. It was only later, when I noticed a sizeable tuft of fur on the floor of the closet, that I realized I had been standing on the tip of her tail.

It has been a harrowing week for Kitty, but she's recovering nicely. I came home from a SISTAs Women's Ministry meeting Sunday evening to find David lying on the couch watching TV and Kitty lying on his legs, asleep. Maybe I've been using the wrong approach – maybe it's trauma and not treats that will turn her into a lap cat.

Chapter 22

Kitty, the Fickle Feline — 9/18/16

Roget's Thesaurus shows a number of synonyms for the word fickle: inconsistent, changeable, unpredictable, picky, and choosy among others. Any of these words describes Kitty, especially the last week when we've been away a lot playing with Spike. For new readers who don't know who that is, Spike is a Great Pyrenees mix who likes for us to come over for a visit when his people are out of town.

Kitty has become so domesticated that we feel comfortable leaving her on her own while we house sit. We are close enough to drop in a couple of times a day, and as long as her food, water, and litter box are in good shape, she seems perfectly happy to be mistress of the manor in our absence.

She does show some signs of loneliness, or so I'm told. As summer comes to an end, fall activities kick in at the church where I work part time. This means letters to participants, Facebook and email updates, newspapers ads, bulletins and bulletin boards, and other assorted duties of a secretary/go-to person. Due to my increased workload and the fact that we now have satellite internet with unlimited on-line access at home, David has been dropping me off at work on his way to check on Kitty and staying there until time to pick me up instead of spending the day at the office with me, using the church internet connection. That means that, when Kitty is at her neediest, he's there and I'm not.

In an earlier chapter, I wrote about the campaign I launched some time ago to encourage Kitty to become more of a lap cat. She now lies on the couch at David's feet when he watches TV or lounges on the end table or ottoman next to my chair while I write, but she avoids actually crawling into our laps like many cats do. When we try to pet her, she often responds with small bites or gentle swats with her claws. I've been told those are expressions of love, but regardless of her intentions, they tend to discourage physical contact.

The exception is when we come home or when we first wake up in the morning. Although she still is not a lap sitter, she persistently rubs our legs and allows us to lean down and pet her – as long as we don't try to pick her up. Apparently, that has all changed, at least where David is concerned.

When he has picked me up this week, he has regaled me with tales of how she jumped into his lap while he was working at his computer desk. It's true that she doesn't usually stay more than three or four minutes, but it still seems unfair. I have been working for a while to make her comfortable, luring her with treats that she only gets if she comes into my lap. She will come and stay as long as the treats last, but once they're gone, so is she. Even then, petting is discouraged.

To add insult to injury, one day last week while I was not there, she actually allowed David to pick her up and sit down with her in his lap for a few minutes. On Friday, we went by the house after he picked me up because I needed some things for weekend meals. Kitty met me at the door with signs that she was glad to see me, so I leaned down and attempted to pick her up. She immediately rolled over and assumed a defensive position, claws and all, so I left her there and went into the kitchen.

That fickle little feline waltzed over to David and began rubbing against his legs. He leaned down, picked her up, and sat down on the couch. As she settled into his lap, they both looked at me with a "Nyah, nyah, nyah" look on their faces. I may have to visit the animal shelter and bring home a dog.

Chapter 23

Cat TV – 10/2/16

I first heard the phrase "cat TV" from Jackson Galaxy on his show, "My Cat from Hell." He was referring to the practice of providing a window seat of some kind for indoor cats so they can watch the outside world in safety. Kitty would have been more accurately described as being from Purgatory rather than from Hell, but the same principals applied. Either way, we were in the process of socializing her, so we cleared some surfaces, made a few furniture adjustments, and gave her access to all the windows in the main living area except the one over the kitchen sink. She has whiled away many afternoons, perched on her Kitty condo or on various pieces of furniture, watching local wildlife and passing neighbors.

I'm aware that cat TV has evolved along with the rest of the world as all of us have become more centered around the electronic world of cyberspace, but a recent Facebook post cast a new perspective on the feline entertainment. A series of fifteen photos was titled "Then vs. Meow – How Technology Has Changed Cats' Lives." The first photo was a two-panel cartoon. The first one showed a cat sleeping on top of an old-fashioned television set – a warm three-foot cube that was perfect for cat naps. The second pictured a cat draped uncomfortably over the top of a modern thin-screened model that was not made for napping.

Many years ago, I had a cat who had an interest in watching television, at least when the weather forecast was on. For those of my readers who are too young to remember, the radar in those days was a round screen with a radial arm that swept around the circle revealing any storms that might be in the area. The map was a non-digital wall map the meteorologist had prepared in advance, and he used a long pointer to draw his viewers' attention to various features. When T.J., my cat, heard the sounds of the weather report, he would run from wherever he was and plant himself in front of the screen. When the radar was on, he would rotate his head in a circle, following the sweeping arm, and when the map was in use, he would stand on his back legs and paw at the pointer. Sometimes he would jump on top of the set or go around behind it looking for the toys that he couldn't quite reach.

Kitty hasn't shown any interest in the weather, but she does occasionally show an interest when David flips to the NatGeo Channel. Being a modern girl, though, she seems more interested in my laptop and my cell phone. More than once I have had to correct my work in progress after she walks across my keyboard, and once I found her frantically pawing at my phone as Siri asked her over and over how she could help.

One of my cousins has several cats, and to say they are spoiled would be a great understatement. She frequently posts videos of her fur babies playing with a new toy or watching a new nature video. One Saturday a couple of weeks ago, Kitty was being particularly rambunctious, running from one end of the house to the other, up and over anything in her path. I wondered how she would react to some digital cat TV, so I Googled bird videos for cats – it's amazing how many there are – and set one to play on my laptop.

At the sound of the first chirp, Kitty's ears perked up, and she hopped onto my ottoman to investigate. She sat watching curiously for a few minutes, but unlike my cousin's cats, she didn't settle down with her paws crossed in a ladylike posture. Instead, she began stalking the birds on the screen. First, she took a closer look by standing on the keyboard. I don't know what she hit, but she managed to freeze the program, and I had to close it and restart it. I tried a squirrel video the second time, but when she began scratching the screen trying to reach the furry critter, video time came to a quick end.

Thankfully, the brief movie break served the purpose of settling Kitty down. Once the screen went black, she jumped up onto her Kitty condo and took a nap. Since then, she has seemed content with cat TV outside the windows. If she becomes bored with the programming and wants to venture back into cyberspace, she'll have to gather up the pennies she sometimes knocks off the dresser and buy her own laptop.

Chapter 24

People Food – 11/6/16

After several weeks of more serious columns, it's time for a Kitty update. Her fans will be glad to know that she's doing well. She has us trained to the point that we rarely resort to spraying her with a water bottle.

She's becoming more social, although it would be a stretch to say that she has become a lap cat. She occasionally jumps into David's lap when he's on his computer, but that's usually because she wants to get from there to the desk so she can investigate all the papers and other interesting gadgets. She allows him to pick her up now and then, too. The other day she actually sat in his lap long enough for me to get a picture as proof.

She still avoids my lap, but she tolerates my petting while she investigates what I have just put in her bowl. She does crawl onto my chest when I go to bed at night because she has learned that I always have a few treats in my hand. She sits quietly and even purrs a bit, but as soon as the last treat is gone, so is she.

She sleeps at my feet most nights, but I don't fool myself that her choice of spots indicates any great affection for me. It's just that, with eleven inches difference in our heights, there's more room at my feet than at David's. Besides, it makes it convenient for her to wake me by chewing on my toes when she's ready for breakfast.

Even though she's into her second years, she's still a growing girl. I'm not sure how much she weighs, but when she stretches out completely, she's over a yard long. I don't think we over feed her. Other than the treats I give her at bedtime, all we give her is a slightly rounded one-third cup of food twice a day. We've avoided giving her people food except for an occasional kernel of popcorn or something that has jumped off the cutting board while I'm preparing dinner. Her normal reaction has been to sniff suspiciously and then walk off with her nose and her tail in the air – until I baked banana bread.

Last week I had a couple of bananas on the counter that had reached that stage of ripeness where the fragrance fills the house, and not in a pleasant way. Once the bread was in the oven, David commented favorably on the new aroma, but Kitty was oblivious – at first. Then, one morning while David was sitting on the couch drinking a cup of coffee, I took him a slice. She was no longer oblivious.

First, her ears and eyes appeared over the edge of the coffee table where he had set the plate. She looked a lot like a "Kilroy was here" graffiti from the World War II era. Then, she put her paws on the table and leaped onto the forbidden surface. No amount of scolding deterred her until David reached for the water bottle.

Finally, he relented and put a small crumb on his leg. She sniffed it, and then, instead of walking away, she nibbled it until it was gone. After that, any time he had banana bread, she had to have a taste. I don't think she was doing any damage to her girlish figure, though. She only wanted the tiniest piece. Once, after she had visited David, she came to see if my banana bread was any better than his. I pinched off a crumb about a quarter inch in diameter and put it on a piece of paper on the floor. She chewed a tiny bit and then left the rest in crumbles spread out all over the paper.

Kitty is unusual in several ways – she's not affected by catnip, she doesn't particularly like being petted, and she seems to prefer dry cat food to anything else we have to offer. It's just as well. Based on how aggressive as she is about the banana bread, if she really liked people food, we'd have to eat in the closet.

Chapter 25

Kitty's New Year's Resolution — 1/8/17

Kitty was a happy cat. She had food and water, two litter boxes, the run of the house, and two humans at her beck and call. With the exception of not being allowed to go outside as often as she would have liked, her life was perfect. No changes were needed, so no resolutions were necessary – and then I made THE VIDEO!

Anyone with a smart phone and a Facebook account has learned, either from the experience of friends or from first-hand experience, the heartache that can result from the indiscreet use of the little camera that is always at your fingertips. A few days before Christmas, I was reading in my favorite chair, and Kitty was rolling around on the floor at my feet. I'm not sure if she was simply enjoying herself or if she was flirting with me. Either way, she caught my attention, and I turned on the video camera.

For the next ninety seconds, she rolled around and acted cute. She ended up on her side where she grabbed her back feet with her front paws and began cleaning her toes. The problem came when the right rear foot refused to cooperate. It worked its way out of the circle and began scratching her ear. She grabbed the errant limb and bit it a couple of times before it escaped again. After repeating the cycle half a dozen times, she gave up, stretched out, and I turned off the camera. Of course, I had to post the results.

Kitty has quite a following, so her video received lots of views and quite a few comments. Surprisingly, the comments were not about how cute or funny she was but about her size. Here are a few examples along with my responses:

A second cousin: She's gotten big!

Me: Yes, she's probably over a yard long when she stretches out, and I'd guess she weighs close to 15 pounds.

Another second cousin: Are you sure you're feeding that cat enough?!?

Me: She doesn't eat that much, but since I don't let her outside anymore, she doesn't get much exercise!

One of David's high school friends: She's quite a porker.

Me: She looks heavier than she really is. Her fur is really thick and fluffy. That's her story and she's sticking to it!

A cousin: She looks about the size of my Lucy, who is rather "fluffy" also.

Being the insensitive pet parents that we are, David and I decided to weigh her. That in itself was an ordeal since it involved David weighing himself and then picking her up and weighing the two of them. I think I've mentioned how she feels about being picked up – she doesn't like it at all. Then, we added insult to injury by announcing the results in her hearing – a whopping seventeen pounds – and we laughed!

I didn't think much about it until Saturday night when I began a nightly ritual I have developed in an effort to encourage Kitty to be more of a lap cat. Once I was ready for bed, I went into the kitchen and poured eight treats into my left hand. I was a little surprised that Kitty didn't follow me. Usually she rubs against my legs, or sometimes she stands up and puts her paws on the edge of the drawer in an effort to encourage me to hurry – but that night she was nowhere to be seen.

Sometimes she beats me back to the bed, but I was under the covers and leaning back against the headboard before she jumped up, sauntered up my legs, and sat down on my stomach. I put one of the treats into my right hand and held it out to her. She sniffed it and turned her head away. I held it between two fingers and touched it to her lips, but she ignored it. I offered it several more times and finally put it back in my left hand with the other treats and offered them all to her on my open palm. Up to this point she had been purring softly, but she had stopped, and I hadn't noticed.

As I continued to wave the treats under her nose, she began to growl softly, deep in her throat. I teased her about

72

being silly, and suddenly she spat and slapped my hand with her paw. Thankfully, she had her claws sheathed, but I finally got the message. I closed my hand over the offending treats and laid my fist down on the bedspread. She blinked her eyes slowly in satisfaction and lay down on my chest. She stayed there for about thirty seconds, allowing me to scratch her neck a little bit before standing up and strolling to the foot of the bed.

Just before she jumped to the floor, she glanced back over her shoulder with a look that said, *You can't tempt me into breaking my New Year's resolution.* Who knew Kitty had so much self control.

Chapter 26

How Old is Kitty? – 3/19/17

Traditional wisdom tells us that one human year is equal to seven dog years and that the ratio is even higher for cats; however, the Internet says something entirely different. When Kitty came to live with us in June of 2015, we guessed that she was born around May 15. That means she is approaching her second birthday, but I wanted to find out how old she was in "cat years." According to various age calculators for cats, she is anywhere from early teens to late twenties. I guess we'll say she's two years old and leave it at that.

Regardless of the years, she is becoming quite the grown up young lady, at least most of the time. She still sometimes races from one end of the house to the other for no apparent reason, and she occasionally spends a few minutes batting a favorite toy around, but she spends most of her time napping or lounging in her Kitty condo, staring out the window at the latest programs on "cat TV."

Kitty has become much more social as she's aged, but she still wants to socialize on her own terms. She loves to be petted when we first wake up in the morning, when we come in after being gone most of the day, and when she's hungry. She will hop up on the bed, my ottoman, or a TV table to make herself a little more accessible, but she really prefers for us to squat down to her level. She especially likes it when, after I've put food in her bowl, I sit on the floor and pet her while she eats.

Occasionally when she's in a good mood, she will let David pick her up and hold her on his lap. She sits as still as a statue while he pets her, then after about thirty seconds, she hops down. On the other hand, if I try to do the same thing, she hisses, spits, and hits the floor running.

She enjoys the treats I give her at bedtime, but I'm not sure how much she enjoys the petting she's required to endure in order to get them. She knows the routine, though. When I go in to brush my teeth, she follows me and lies on the floor. After

I'm finished, I head for the kitchen where I keep her treats, and she usually beats me there. So far, she hasn't knocked me off my feet on the way, but she has come close. She watches me intently while I count out the appropriate number of little crunchy bits, and then she races me for the bed. She's usually sitting expectantly by my pillow before I make it back to the bedroom, and I sometimes have to fight for space to get under the covers.

She sits nicely on my stomach or chest, whichever will cause me the most discomfort. I sit back against the headboard and feed her the treats one at a time, stroking her back or scratching her neck while she chews. She tolerates the stroking and even purrs a little bit once in a while, but if I linger too long, she whips her head around and glares at the offending hand threateningly.

Other changes in the routine upset her, too. Once I switched hands so I was holding the treats in my right hand and petting her with my left. A hiss and a swat with her paw put a quick end to that experiment. Regardless of how closely I stick to the rules, she's gone as soon as she swallows the last treat.

Several times recently she has lingered a little while. Sometimes she rubs her face against the book I'm reading, and on rare occasions, she lies beside me for a few minutes – close but not touching. At first, I thought my togetherness campaign was working, but I came to realize she was just hanging around in case I discovered some extra treats hidden away. I guess I'm okay with that. At her age, she's old enough to decide how much she wants to give to this relationship.

Chapter 27

Kitty: When She's Good — 4/9/17

Henry Wadsworth Longfellow wrote a poem called "There was a little girl." For those who don't remember it, here's the first verse:

> There was a little girl,
> And she had a little curl
> Right in the middle of her forehead.
> When she was good
> She was very, very good,
> And when she was bad she was horrid.

That describes Kitty – not the curl, of course, but the good and the bad – especially during and after a week of being left on her own.

David and I recently spent a week playing with Spike, our big dog friend. Kitty doesn't go with us anymore when we house sit, because she was not very well behaved the last time she visited. She's very self reliant at home as long as we leave her with a clean litter box and a full bowl. Apparently, though, she get's lonely.

After taking care of Spike's needs each morning, David would drop me off at the church, and he would go to the house, check the mail, and tend to Kitty's needs. Even though she's still somewhat anti-social, being alone for most of the time made her much more friendly. She rubbed against David's legs, almost tripping him up more than once, and she jumped up on the couch next to him. She even tolerated being picked up and held in his lap, sometimes for as long as a minute or two.

David is still Kitty's favorite, but when our house sitting gig was over and we both returned home, she was even affectionate to me. She would jump up on my ottoman several times a day and stand still while I petted her, and she tolerated being brushed once in a while. Every night I woke up with her sleeping at my feet instead of just every now and then. Believe it or not, I have even been allowed to scratch her neck from time to time.

That's the good part. The bad part is that she learned a new way to get into mischief while she was home alone.

The first clue I noticed was a dead bug or two and some bits of other twiggy-looking things on the stove and surrounding countertop. It had been windy, so I assumed I was seeing debris that had been blown down the exhaust fan (country roofs get very dirty). Nothing else on the cabinet had been disturbed, so no other possibility occurred to me. Then, one day I walked into the kitchen and knew something wasn't right.

Our kitchen cabinets stop about a foot shy of the ceiling, and there's a small strip of molding around the top. The molding is strictly decorative and it's not expected that there will be any traffic way up there, so it's only held on by a couple of staples and some glue. That day, however, the strip on the cabinet beside the sink wasn't being held in place by much of anything except one lone staple. It was suspended at a crazy angle, resting against an angel that hangs on the side of the cabinet. I pointed it out to David, and we both knew immediately what had caused it. (Apparently, the molding hides dead bugs and other twiggy things, too.)

That night, David and I were in bed reading when I heard an unfamiliar sound from the kitchen. It took a few seconds for the sound to penetrate past the plot of the latest thriller that had my attention. When it finally did, I put down my book and listened.

"That sounded like a cat jumping up on the cabinets," I said.

Either David's book is much more engrossing than mine or he has never listened with a parent's ears. "What?" he said.

I climbed out of bed and headed for the kitchen. I flipped on the light, and there she was, staring down at me from her perch several feet above the countertops, and looking very pleased with herself. I hurried back to the bedroom and grabbed the squirt bottle full of water that we use for disciplinary purposes. Back in the kitchen, I didn't see her at first, but then she peeked out from behind the canning pot that stays above the microwave. My first shot caught her in the face, and she backtracked to the corner. I hit her with several more good squirts before she jumped down to the stovetop and took off for parts unknown.

I didn't hear much out of her for the rest of the night, but by morning, she was sitting by the food bowl, waiting for her breakfast. Since then, I've seen a bit more dust on the countertop a couple of times, but she has saved her antics for her alone times, so there's not much I can do. Besides, she's still being pretty good most of the time, and I'll settle for that.

Chapter 28

Kitty: Interior Designer — 4/23/17

Saturday morning was project time around our house. The first project was in the dining room and the second was in the bedroom – and Kitty was right in the middle of both of them.

The dining room task involved a new table and chairs, or new to us anyway. After David's mother passed away, his sister inherited a good deal of her furniture. Sentiment only goes so far when it comes to decorating tastes, so she recently asked David if we would like to have the dining table and chairs. Since what we had was really too big for our dining area and didn't match the built-in hutch very well, he said yes.

The problem is that a table, two leafs, and six chairs won't fit in the back of a Grand Prix, so David began looking for alternatives. Since we can't pull a trailer either, he checked on renting a van. After the sticker shock wore off, he asked our friend Kent if we could borrow his truck. Kent had another idea, and Friday the two of them left before dawn pulling a small enclosed trailer in case it rained. They planned to be back by 4:00, but I guess traffic was heavy because by the time they pulled into the driveway, they barely had time to unload the truck and make it to Home Group Bible Study.

They hadn't exactly thrown the furniture through the door, but the chairs had been placed at odd angles in odd places, the table legs that were wrapped in a quilt were piled next to the couch, and the table top was upside down in the middle of the living room. Kitty loved it! First, she sniffed every chair from top to bottom – then, she curled up on the table top in one of the corners where a leg would go and went to sleep.

The next morning, David put the table together – with Kitty's help – and I helped set the chairs in place. Then, I moved on to the bedroom where I had some new curtains to hang. While I ironed the creases out of the panels, Kitty hid among the trailing ends and jumped out to chase the cord of the iron. As I laid each panel out flat on the bed, she insisted on lying on each one. I sighed at the thought of her long black hair on the eggshell-colored fabric. David helped me mount the hardware, and the curtains were soon installed with no further incident.

I warmed up some leftover spaghetti from Home Group, and we enjoyed lunch on our new dining room furniture. I was cleaning up the kitchen – my last job before an afternoon of working on my latest book project – when I heard Kitty crying. I knew something was wrong, because she rarely makes a sound, so I went running. She was under the table, hanging by one paw, and struggling to get away. One of her claws was caught on something where the leg joins the table, and she couldn't get it loose. I tried to help, but she let me know that my help was not appreciated. David arrived about the time she managed to work her claw free, and she took off for wherever she goes when she disappears.

All three of us spent the afternoon taking it easy. I worked on my computer, David provided a continuous line-up of movies for our viewing pleasure, and once she reappeared, Kitty slept. She didn't seem to be suffering from any permanent damage, but she hovered close to one of us, lying first on my ottoman and then moving across the room to lie at David's feet on the couch. She also napped for a while on a stack of folded quilts and moving blankets that were waiting to be moved back into the shed. The one thing she didn't do was venture anywhere close to the dining table. I guess her designing days are over for a while.

Chapter 29

Anywhere She Wants — 5/28/17

There's an old joke that poses the questions "Where does a 900-pound gorilla sleep?" The answer, of course, is "anywhere he wants to." That same principle applies in the Brendle household. The last time we managed to wrangle Kitty onto the scale, she only weighed in at fourteen pounds, but she still sleeps anywhere she wants to.

I set a bad precedence shortly after she evolved from being an under-the-porch stray to queen of the castle. When she showed an interest in the TV table formerly known as my computer desk, I moved the computer to my ottoman or my lap. It is, after all, a laptop. We also cleared off various surfaces to allow her a clear view out the windows, and she was satisfied with her territory for a while. Lately, though, I've noticed subtle encroachments taking place.

First, it was David's chair at the dinner table. After he finishes his meal, he always takes his plate to the sink and goes into the bedroom to get his evening vitamins while I get the ice cream (there's always room for Blue Bell). One night not long ago, as soon as he left the table, Kitty hopped up into his chair and made herself comfortable. When he came back, he sweet-talked her a little and tilted the chair slightly. She ignored him, though, and rather than press the issue, he pulled another chair up beside her and sat down. The same thing happened the next night except that he skipped the sweet talk and went straight to the other chair. It seems that I'm not the only enabler in the family.

As for me, Kitty apparently wasn't satisfied with displacing me from the TV table because she soon set her sights on the ottoman, too. Several nights ago I sat down to do some writing, and I moved my computer from the ottoman to my lap. Kitty immediately moved into the empty spot, stretched out, and promptly went to sleep. When I finished for the evening, I didn't want to disturb her, so I found a new computer resting place. We'll see how long she allows me to keep this one.

The final invasion of occupied space came in the bed. When we settle down for the night, Kitty sometimes wanders the house for a while, but if or when she decides to join us in bed, she usually sleeps on my side at the end of the bed. There's more room there than on David's side. One night, though, while we were still reading, she found a spot on the turned down comforter on David's side, and she looked as if she intended to stay there.

"Now where am I supposed to put my feet, Kitty?" he asked. She didn't respond, so I did.

"How about on my side," I suggested.

So that's what we did. I turned on my side and pulled my knees up in my normal sleeping position. David turned corner to corner and straightened his legs so his feet were below mine. We slept that way for a while, at least until Her Majesty decided to leave the bed to us commoners while she wandered around the house.

There's no great purpose to this story except to show how well-trained David and I are. Kitty continues to try out new sleeping spots, but she releases them back to us once she's reminded us who is really in charge around here – and once she's established once again that she can sleep anywhere she wants.

Chapter 30

Kitty Loves Us — 8/20/17

I decided early in the week to make Kitty the focus of this column. Before I sat down at the keyboard, I consulted the Internet about the meaning of a couple of her idiosyncrasies that I intended to write about. What I found was an article written in 2014 by Modi Ramoson titled "9 Signs Your Cat Actually Loves You." It provided some very interesting insights into Kitty's behavior.

1. Your cat brings you their "presents" - When your cat brings you their kill it is actually meant as a present...a love token.

Thankfully, Kitty is an indoor cat, so her presents consist of various toys. Her favorite at the moment is a yellow stuffed elephant. It frequently ends up at David's feet when he's sitting on the couch or on my side of the bed when it's time to make it up.

2. Your kitty will flash you their tummy - If your cat rolls over on its back to give you a flash of that fuzzy belly...they feel comfortable around you...they feel loved and protected by you.

Kitty loves to show us her tummy. She frequently makes quite a production of rolling over, all the while watching us to see if we think she's cute. It's a completely different story, though, if we try to rub or scratch her belly. That is forbidden!

3. Your cat has a thing for head butting you - To receive a head butt from a cat is a pretty big deal...leaving traces of their scent to claim you.

Kitty doesn't head butt either of us, but she will touch her nose to mine if I catch her in the right mood. The contact is not really close enough to leave much of a scent, but she does sniff my breath as if she's trying to figure out if I've eaten anything interesting recently.

4. Love bites... but hopefully not too hard! - When your cat nibbles on you playfully, this is one of their ways of showing their affections towards you...more than anything.

I didn't catch on to this one for a while. If Kitty was lying on a raised surface and I walked by, she often reached out and grabbed my hand. If she caught it, she bit, and I made it worse by jerking away and dragging my hand across a tooth. Lately I've changed my reaction, and it's easy to see what Ramoson meant. When I let her have my hand, she sniffs, licks a finger or two, and sometimes gently captures one between her teeth. Then, she loses interest and releases me unharmed – and she doesn't get yelled at – a win for both sides.

5. Following/Lingering around wherever you are - Cats often linger around their owners when they are fond of them...rubbing around their legs...accidentally tripping them as they walk. Know that they are only doing this because they want to be close to you.

This sign definitely describes Kitty. David and I have both, at one time or another, almost hit the floor as she rubbed against our legs or chased our feet when we were walking. She also likes to rub my legs when I'm in the kitchen, although I'm not sure that's so much out of affection as it is hope that I might have a little extra milk that might end up in her bowl.

6. Kneading their master - If your cat kneads you like pizza dough, this is really their way of showing you the love they developed as babies when nursing from their mothers.

Kitty doesn't qualify under this sign - it requires a closeness that she is not fond of. I'm not upset about it, though. I've had a kneading cat before, and if they still have their claws, it can be a very painful experience.

7. Twitching the tips of their tail - If your cat holds their tail up casually, flipping the tip when they're around you, they think you're the "cat's meow."

Kitty is definitely a tail flipper! Even if she's lying down with her eyes closed, she flips the end of her tail if we say her name.

8. The power of the purr - If kitty happens to purr loudly every time you pay them some attention, this is a very good sign they've developed special feelings for you.

Aside from the day she walked out from under the porch squalling at the top of her lungs, Kitty has never been very vocal. She sometimes "chirps" at a bug outside the window, and she scolds her elephant in a very quiet trill when it jumps off the bed without her permission. She also purrs occasionally when chewing on her bedtime snacks, but that is more of a silent vibration than a real purr. Other than those few instances, she's the strong, silent type and shows her feelings in other ways.

9. Eye contact with a kitty kiss - Cats only tend to make eye contact with those they know well and have developed trust for – so if you catch your kitty giving you the eye, don't be worried. When your kitty locks eyes with you, casting a slow blink once eyes are met, this is their version of a kiss. Be a sweetie and give them a slow blink in return.

This sign was totally new to me, but it's now my favorite. Frequently, when Kitty is lying on one of her perches across the room, I will realize she's staring at me. When I return her gaze, she doesn't look away, and if I call her name, she does the slow blink. Who knew it was a Kitty kiss!

Since Kitty has become a full-time indoor cat, I have fretted about the fact that she's not a lap cat. I tried all sorts of techniques to entice her to become a more cuddly ball of fur, but she hasn't really changed that much other than to sit really close to David occasionally or stand on his legs now and then. Still, after reading this list, I now realize that Kitty loves us – she really loves us!

Chapter 31

Kitty Missed Us — 9/17/17

In the previous chapter, I shared a list of ways to know if your cat really loves you. After comparing the list with Kitty's behavior, I decided that she really does love us – sometimes David more than me, but I'm mostly okay with that. Taking my cue from the list, I've been responding in a more feline manner, and she has become a little more affectionate toward me.

For instance, when I walk by her and she grabs for my hand, instead of jerking away from her, I now stop and hold my hand still. She will hold it gently between her paws and sniff to see what interesting things I have been up to. Then, she'll either lick my finger or hold it between her teeth. Sometimes, she'll let me scratch under her chin a bit, but I don't press my luck. If I linger too long, she gets frisky and begins to bite. She seems to appreciate the interaction, and she has started following me around almost as much as she does David.

That made it a little hard to leave her when we decided to spend a long weekend in Arkansas with my brother and sister-in-law. We've left her before, and she does fine – but this time, she knew something was up. She took turns sitting in our suitcases, and she stuck even closer than usual to one or the other of us. I knew she would miss us more this time.

We had a great time in Arkansas, but I couldn't help but wonder what waited for us when we got home. I once had a cocker spaniel who, when he was upset with me, caught hold of an end of the toilet paper between his teeth and ran from one end of the house to the other. I shuddered to think what kind of chaos Kitty could cause if she decided to punish us.

On the other hand, there are more subtle methods of getting even. When my son was a toddler, my parents would often call mid-week to ask if we had plans for the weekend that would require overnight child care for him. Of course, they were more than happy to offer their services. He always had a great time with his grandparents, but he was always exited to see me – at least at first. When I first stepped out of the car, his eyes would light up and he would flash me a big smile. Then, as if it had suddenly occurred to him that I had left him, the smile would fade and he would turn his face away. For a little while, he wouldn't have anything to do with me, and I wondered if I would receive the same treatment from Kitty.

We arrived home from our trip after four and a half days, and Kitty was on the arm of the recliner waiting to greet us as we walked in the door. She was glad to see us, and she demanded almost constant petting for the first few hours. After that, she was less demanding, but she still wanted to be close to one of us. A quick inspection of the house showed nothing out of order except for a few black hairs on the kitchen counter and an air freshener that had been knocked over, so I guess we escaped retribution this time.

The first item on the list of ways to know if your cat really loves you is that she will bring you gifts. I mentioned that Kitty often brings her favorite toy, a small stuffed elephant, to David and drops it at his feet. I have to admit that I sometimes feel a little jealous that she doesn't show the same generosity to me. However, the morning after we arrived home, some time before the sun came up, I felt her jump up on my side of the bed. She carefully picked her way through the tangle of blankets and feet and stopped at the edge of my pillow. Then, she dropped her elephant on my face and lay down against my legs. Yes, I'm pretty sure she missed us.

Chapter 32

National Cat Day – 10/29/17

Sunday was National Cat Day. I had no idea there was such a day until one of my Facebook friends posted a picture of her cat in celebration of the holiday. I went to Google to find out what this special day was all about, and I found a website with, among other things, an article giving 20 ways to celebrate. I was disappointed when I realized that at least 10 of the way involved buying products from the company that sponsors the website and probably the day itself. I decided I'd celebrate in my own way – by writing about the feline I know best – Kitty.

Kitty has gone through a few changes lately. During a recent stop at one of the dollar stores in town, I found a toy I thought she would like. It's a small stuffed fish attached to a pole by an elastic cord. It's similar to a toy she had when she was new to the Brendle household. She liked to chase it when one of us bounced it around, but her favorite thing to do was to drag it around the house with the pole trailing behind her. She eventually chewed through the string, but the fish was still her constant companion. At some point, she stuffed it under or inside something where I can't find it and neither can she, because it hasn't been seen for months.

In its absence, she transferred her attention to a stuffed elephant. She would bring it to David several times a day as a token of her affections, and she brought it to me once in a while so I wouldn't feel completely left out.

When I brought home the new fish toy, I dangled it in front of her, and she played with it like she did when she was a kitten. When she tired of that game, she picked up the fish in her mouth and wandered off with the pole dragging behind her. I haven't seen much of it since then. I catch a glimpse of it now and then against a wall or under a table, but it's not her constant companion like the first one was. The odd thing is that she now completely ignores the elephant. Maybe her dwindling attachment to her toys is due to her increasing affection for

David. Kitty has always preferred David, but recently she has exhibited some possessivness along with her preference.

We gave up satellite TV a while back, and a few weeks ago David subscribed to a streaming service that brings our TV reception through the Internet. It's much less expensive than satellite, and it works well – most of the time. Unfortunately, there are problems with our favorite channel, and when we're watching our "special" programs, the reception is often intermittent. The provider says they're "working on it," but for now, when it happens, we access the program on one of our laptops or David's tablet where the reception is better. The only problem is that, in order for both of us to see the smaller screen, we have to sit next to each other on the couch. Since we like each other pretty well, that's not a hardship, but it seems to be a problem for Kitty.

Last week we were watching NCIS, and she stalked over to the couch, sat down at my feet, and stared at me. I invited her to join us, but she didn't respond. I repeated the invitation a couple of times until she took a swipe at me with claws extended and stalked away. Sunday night we were watching another program on David's tablet, and she took up her vigil at my feet again. This time when I invited her up, she accepted. I was working on my columns during commercials, and she investigated my laptop for a few minutes while she allowed me to pet her. When she'd had enough of my attention, she bared her teeth in the direction of my hand and jumped down.

David thinks I'm imagining things when I say she's jealous, but after she left me, she walked around the coffee table and sat down in front of him. Maybe it's a woman thing, but I recognized the look in her eyes as she stared at him. She was saying, "How could you? My place is next to you on the couch, and you let HER sit there!" Besides, this is not the only situation in which she's exhibited her displeasure.

With the cooler weather, I've pulled a few jackets out of the back of the closet. The day the temperature dipped into the 30s, I put on a pullover fleece that I've had for several years. Apparently some of the old thread had given way allowing the tag to rub against the back of my neck. I didn't want to mess up my hair by removing the jacket, so I asked David if he could cut it out for me. He was glad to help, but since his eyes aren't as young as they used to be, he suggested that we go over by the dining room windows so he could see better.

Now, those windows are one of Kitty's favorite spots to sit and watch the wildlife that frequents our back yard. It's also close to the dining table where David sits to use his computer, so I'm guessing she considers it one of "their" spots. Regardless of her motivation, she ran over to where we were standing, sat down at our feet, and scolded us for several seconds before leaving in a huff. She's rarely vocal, so her conversation wasn't just simple small talk.

Although it's interesting to speculate, what she's feeling won't change the way David and I relate to each other. On the other hand, there was a time when we declared that we didn't want a house cat, and look where we are now. Even though Sunday was National Cat Day, it wasn't all that different from any other day for us. In the Brendle house, every day is Kitty Day.

Chapter 33

Kitty Dislikes Changes, Too — 12/10/17

Change is one of those things that few people are neutral about – they either thrive on the new and different or they cling to the old and familiar. I'm more of a clinger. I tend to buy the same brands when I shop, I avoid trendy fashions in favor of the classics, and I almost never rearrange my furniture. This week, however, I've had to adjust.

David's sister has ordered a new sofa and is passing on the sofa and love seat that were originally in their mother's house to us. Since we have no extra space in either the house or the storage shed, our existing sofa, chair, and recliner have to go. I took pictures of those pieces shortly after we returned from our Thanksgiving visit with David's family, but for some reason – probably my resistance to change – I didn't follow through and post them on the Rains County On-Line Garage Sale. Last Friday, I finally got busy, and within four hours of my posting, the recliner was gone. Less than twenty-four hours later, the sofa and chair were sold, and by the time this column is published, they will be gone, too.

Kitty always hides when anyone new comes into the house, but as soon as the family who bought the recliner hauled it out the door, she came in to inspect the empty spot. I have to admit that it wasn't completely empty considering the dust bunnies and dead bugs that were under it, but that just added interest to her inspection tour. She was still interested Saturday morning, and when I dragged out the seldom used steam iron to coax the matted carpet back to its original fluffiness, she watched closely, just to make sure I did it right.

About the time she was becoming accustomed to the blank spot in the living room, David filled it with the rocking chair from the bedroom, and she had to begin again. First, she had to give her approval to the new placement in the living room, and then she had to thoroughly inspect the now empty spot in the bedroom. It was an exhausting job, and she took a long nap afterward. She will be really worn out when the dramatic changes that are in her future occur.

The changing temperature is something else that neither of us is very enthusiastic about. My preferred footwear is none, so I don't like it when the tile floor begins to get cold and I have to go back to wearing house shoes – and I hate it when the bathrooms feel like meat lockers! Kitty doesn't seem too crazy about it this year either.

After spending half of her first winter outside, she seemed to find the indoor climate too warm for her taste. She preferred lying on the tile rather than the carpet, and she avoided sitting in front of the heater or lying in the sunshine. That seems to have changed as she approaches her third winter. Since the temperature has dropped, her favored napping spots are the end of the bed or snuggled down into David's afghan on the sofa. This weekend I saw her lying at the very edge of the oscillating heater's range, and later on, she stretched out in a patch of sunshine that was streaming through the storm door.

She has also decided that sleeping alone at night is a cold and lonely proposition. Several times lately, I've awakened during the night to find her pressed against my stomach. As I said earlier, I don't take to change easily. With her in front and David snuggled up against my back, it's warm – very warm – and it's also a bit hard to breath and almost impossible to move. One night I had a cramp in my leg and was frantic to change positions. Considering the weight difference between Kitty and David, she was the one that had to move, and she ended up on the floor. She didn't seem to mind too much, though. The next night she was back.

Kitty and I are both going to have to adjust to new furniture, and I guess I'll have to adjust to the new sleeping arrangements. After all, I've been hoping she would become more of a lap cat, and this may be as close as she gets.

The Princess and the Kitty Bed – 1/7/18

It's no secret that Kitty is spoiled and that she reigns in the Brendle home, but I don't think I realized how true that is until this past weekend. The fairy tale of the "Princess and the Pea" is not much of a tale compared with "The Princess and the Kitty Bed."

When Kitty first began to sleep in the laundry room on cold nights, I folded an old mattress pad and put it in a laundry basket on top of the dryer for her. It gave her a place off the cold tile and away from the draft that crept in under the door. There was always a Kitty shaped depression in the middle of it along with an abundance of her excess fur each morning, so I assumed it met with her approval.

Later, as she worked her way further into our hearts and our home, she abandoned her laundry basket but never seemed to settle on a particular sleeping place. On one of my frequent trips to the pet department, I bought her a cushy little bed covered in blue and gray velour. I thought it was a bed fit for a princess, but she didn't agree.

I tried everything to lure her to try it out, convinced that once she snuggled into it, she wouldn't want to leave it. I placed it in some of her favorite sleeping places – halfway between the dining room and the living room, on top of the cedar chest, and even under our bed. She ignored it. I sprinkled it with catnip to no avail. I even spread a few of her favorite snacks in it, but she managed to snag the goodies without getting into the bed.

For a year or so, the bed has lingered in limbo while she explored other places to lie down. She can be found lounging in her Kitty condo or a dining chair staring out the window into the back yard. She has recently adopted the foot of our bed as her own and sometimes creeps up to lie against me if she's particularly cold or lonely. Her favorite place, though, is the end of the couch where David sits or lies down to watch TV. She particularly likes to nestle into the crocheted afghan when it's folded into a neat square, but she will lie against David's leg if he's using the afghan to ward off a chill. I'm not sure if he's the attraction or if it's the edge of the afghan she's after, but either way, they're both happy.

Then Christmas came. A week or so before the big day, a large box from Amazon arrived on our front porch. Our son had told us to expect a gift and had said it would be wrapped so we could open the shipping box. The gift was in a large red bag made of shiny red satiny fabric, and Kitty was fascinated. She didn't damage it, but she returned to it repeatedly to sniff and rub against it. On Christmas morning the bag was removed to reveal an Instant Pot Multi-Function Cooker, and the bag was abandoned on the floor.

At least it was abandoned until Kitty discovered it lying there. Several times during the day I noticed her investigating it, inside and out, or lying on it looking smugly comfortable. Later, after lunch with Aunt Fay, I was straightening the living room, and I picked up the bag, wondering what to do with it. I hated to throw it away, so I put it on the afghan on the couch. It wasn't long before Kitty way lying, not just on it, but halfway in it, snoozing away.

The red bag stayed there for the next week or so until last Saturday when I decided to do a little more thorough cleaning than usual. I dragged out the heavy vacuum instead of the carpet sweeper, and I moved a few of the lighter items instead of just cleaning around the edges. The lightest item, of course, was the Kitty bed that was always in the way. I picked it up and started to put it on the love seat as usual, but instead I put it on the afghan with the red bag on top of it.

When the cleaning was done, I sat down on the love seat to read for a few minutes, and Kitty jumped up on the couch to rest from dodging the vacuum. She stood looking at the Kitty bed for a few minutes and then crept up on it slowly. She tested it warily with one foot, and when nothing bad happened, she climbed in. Since then, she has spent many happy naps snuggled down. It seems to me that Kitty may suffer from "princess syndrome," but all it took to satisfy Her Furry Highness was red satin sheets.

Kitty's New Game – 3/18/18

Anyone who has pets, especially curious cats, knows that these animals have a thing about closed doors. They have a strong desire to be on the side of the door where they're not. It's the pet version of "the grass is always greener" – that thing that causes cows and horses to stretch their necks between strands of barbed wire to try and reach one scrawny dandelion while standing in a patch of lush green clover. It was also most likely the inspiration behind the invention of the pet door that so many of us have installed in our homes.

This need to be on the other side has resulted in several frayed spots in the carpet at our house where Kitty has tried to dig her way under the offending obstacle. It has also led to the creation of several games. Her favorite – and by far the noisiest – is "Beat David to the Office." Our home is approximately eighty feet long from end to end, with the master bedroom on one end and the office on the other. The office door is one of Kitty's greatest challenges because it's usually closed. In addition, I've put a throw rug across the threshold of the doorway, so she can't even pull threads out of the carpet to express her frustration. But she's always on the alert for a chance to slip into that wonderland of shelves and computer wires. Even if she's asleep on our bed, if David takes a step down the hallway toward the office, she comes thundering through the house – who knew one thirteen-pound cat could sound so much like a stampede – and dashes into the office ahead of him.

Her second favorite game is "The Breakfast Dash." After she has finished her morning jumping jack routine on the bed and I'm sufficiently awake, she hides behind the rocking chair. Once I've found my glasses and house shoes and am moving toward the kitchen, the game begins. The object seems to be to dash out from behind the rocker and to her food bowl without either tripping me or running into the cabinet. Her braking ability is not always great on the tile floor.

She doesn't always want to play "The Breakfast Dash," though. I'm a pretty early riser, and if she's been up roaming the house all night, she sometimes decides to sleep in. On those mornings, I leave the bedroom door ajar slightly so she can open it when she feels the need without announcing her desire by clawing the carpet. Once she has graced me with her presence in the living room, I close the door so the light won't bother David. She's usually okay with that, content to lie on the end table by the love seat where I sit for my morning quiet time.

This past week, however, she disrupted the routine with the introduction of a new game. I think it was Wednesday morning, several days after the time change. She was still sleeping when I woke up coughing and decided to go ahead and get up. She roused enough to watch me go into the kitchen, but since she showed no interest in moving from her warm spot on the bed, I closed the door. It wasn't long before I heard the sound of little fingernails, so I opened the door for Her Majesty. She strolled through with her nose in the air, but the second I started the close the door, she made a beeline for the bedroom. We repeated this little dance step a few times before I finally got smart and left the door ajar. The next time I looked, she was sitting squarely on the threshold, daring me to guess which room she wanted to be in.

I tired of the game before she did and left her standing – or sitting – guard. Her new game isn't any fun without an opponent, so she soon joined me in the living room. Once she was settled by the window, watching whatever it is she sees in the dark, I casually picked up my coffee cup and headed for the kitchen for a refill. Of course, while I was there, I closed the door without interference.

Kitty's new game probably won't win any awards. In fact, I'm not sure it will be popular enough to rate a name. Still, it entertained her for a few minutes, and it gave me some new material, so I guess it's worth an honorable mention.

Kitty's Tolerance is Growing — 4/29/18

One of the author groups I belong to on Facebook asked us to share a brief "getting to know you" post. Here's what I wrote:

> *I retired from the business world ten years ago, but it didn't last. I work part-time at my church, do some on-line accounting for my son's publishing company, and write for our local weekly newspaper. I have one son, two beautiful grandchildren, and an almost domesticated feral cat who loves my husband and tolerates me.*

Kitty and I were making great strides in our relationship until my extended bout with allergies and a sinus infection accompanied by a very persistent and irritating cough. The first issue was that I was miserable and didn't feel like currying the favor of Her Royal Snottiness, so I basically ignored her. I did, however, still offer treats at bedtime, but for some reason, she refused to follow the rules. Instead of lying on my stomach as I required, she insisted on sitting beside me. She didn't even want to get close enough to take the treats out of my lap but instead wanted me to put them in front of her on the bed.

I was in no mood to be manipulated by a temperamental feline, so I refused to relax my standards. The result was that, several times, she left in a huff, leaving me with a handful of tuna-flavored treats. Since David refused to eat them, I gave in, and a new routine developed – she would lie beside me and eat the treats out of my hand, but petting was limited and purely at her discretion.

Sometime in March, my symptoms began to clear up, and although my cough persisted longer than the other symptoms, it became less annoying. Eventually, it disappeared almost completely, and then an amazing thing happened. One evening when Kitty came in for her treats, she put her front paws on my stomach, and when I dropped a treat in front of her, she ate it where it was. Since then, she has gradually moved back to her original place and has even allowed me to resume petting her occasionally.

I have a theory about what may have happened. When the sun goes down, Kitty becomes rather skittish. While we sit in the living room and read or watch TV, she runs from one window to another, checking out various noises and movements she sees or hears. Once we go to bed, she often startles and stares at the window air conditioner as if fearing the appearance of an intruder. My theory is that, since she was already a bit on edge, and since my cough was always worse when I was lying down, she wanted to distance herself as much as possible from the sudden explosive sounds and movements. She didn't want to give up the treats altogether, though, so she offered a compromise which I reluctantly accepted.

I think she missed me, though, because she has found a couple of new opportunities for closeness. For example, she has taken to lying along the back of the love sit where I sit. It's nice because, although she sometimes resists petting, she doesn't seem to mind if I lay my head back against her – and she makes a really nice headrest. Occasionally, she slides down against my shoulders, and it's like having a live heating pad. Still, this arrangement has its drawback. First, she gets heavy after a while, and secondly, she expresses her enjoyment of the arrangement by beating me on the side of the head with her tail.

There are other times when I come into the living room and find her sitting in my spot. Unlike my old chair, there's plenty of room for both of us on the loveseat, and she graciously allows me to sit beside her and even to pet her within limits.

There's probably not an explanation for her change in behavior that makes sense on a human level, but I like to think she's warming up to me. But even if it's just that she's developing a greater level of tolerance as she approaches her third birthday, I can live with that.

Chapter 37

A Tale of Kitty's Tail – 7/29/18

Kitty plays favorites – she's definitely partial to David and spends much more time with him than she does with me. That's not really news, but it continues to be a source of disappointment to me – most of the time.

In the last several months, she has begun to warm up to me more. She sometimes rubs against my legs and then stands with her left rear foot on top of my left foot. I'm not sure exactly what that means, but she does it to David frequently, and it seems to imply some sort of ownership. She's also allowing me to pet her more, and she sometimes asks me for attention, especially when we first get home in the afternoon. If she's awake when we arrive, she greets us from the chair by the front door, pushing her head against any part of us she can reach, especially if it's a hand. She used to save this kind of affection for David, but now I'm included as well.

Another new bid for attention involves my rolling computer stand and the TV table that has become one of her favorite napping places. Because of spatial limitations, the tables are close to each other, and the "mouse ledge" of the computer stand overlaps the edge of the TV table by several inches. When Kitty is lying on her TV table, she rests her head on the computer stand. This is no problem at all except when I'm using my mouse, and Kitty decides she needs my attention. Sometimes she tries to take the mouse out of my hand, and since she doesn't always remember to sheath her claws, this can be painful for me. Other times she will put her paw on my hand and give that I-know-you-want-to-pet-me look. My typical response is to rub just above her eyes with one finger. She likes that until she doesn't, and then she bites me.

For quite some time, one of Kitty's favorite places to lie has been the back of the sofa where David usually sits. It's high enough to allow her to look down on her loyal subjects, and it's close to David. It's also fun to dig between the cushions and the back of the couch unless, of course, David has the spray bottle close at hand to give her a squirt for scratching the furniture. Lately, she has been spending some time on the back of the love seat where I sit. Her favorite place is right behind me. That puts her in the perfect spot to swish her tail and whop me upside my head. Who knew a fluffy tail could pack such a wallop.

Occasionally, instead of lying lengthwise along the back, she lies across it so she can look out the window better. She scoots her backside down until she's sitting on my shoulder. It's nice and cozy, and she allows me to lay my head against her like a pillow. Thankfully, she chooses the left shoulder instead of the sore one (I had rotator cuff issues in 2018), and I enjoy the closeness – until, that is, she swishes her tail. Then, instead of hitting me in the ear, she gets me in the face. Oh well. I guess since I'm number two in her affections, I have to take what I can get, even if it seems like I'm getting the bad end of the deal.

Chapter 38

Kitty's Camping Experience — 8/12/18

After sitting idle in our backyard for six years, we recently began making our motor home road ready – and David was anxious to take a test run to a local campground to see what items other than the refrigerator and generator needed attention. As it turned out, he was more anxious than I thought – last week we spent four days at a Thousand Trails campground near us.

After checking our calendar, scheduling an outing became a now-or-much-later decision since I will be recovering from rotator cuff surgery for the next several weeks. David opted for now, and I began making lists. Sunday after church we shuttled back and forth between the house and the coach with armloads of clothes, food, and Kitty necessities. I almost backed out when David told me that I wouldn't be able to use the refrigerator after all, but I simplified my menu plans and added an ice chest to my list.

One of the first things David did once preparations were underway was to get Kitty's carrier out of the shed. In the interest of safety – both hers and ours – we had agreed that it was not a good idea to let her roam free while the motor home was underway. When he brought the carrier into the house, David put it on top of a box, and Kitty immediately gave it a good sniffing, stretching up on her hind legs to reach it. I put it down on the floor and opened the door, and she went inside and lay down. She was ready to go.

She rode quietly to the campground, but when we arrived and opened her door, she immediately disappeared. After we hooked up the water, electricity, and sewer and put out the slides, I went looking for her. I found her in the bedroom, crouched on a nightstand under a corner of the comforter. We didn't see much of her until bedtime. She wasn't interested in dinner, but when I brushed my teeth, she appeared in the bathroom, waiting expectantly for her nightly treats. After scarfing them down, she spent most of the night snuggled against my legs or lying between David and me.

We decided not to leave her alone in an unfamiliar environment, so Monday morning David dropped me at the church and took Kitty to the house. He said she took about four steps into the living room and collapsed on the floor as if exhausted from her ordeal. That afternoon when the three of us drove back to the campground, she was not quite as ready to go as she had been the day before. David had to coax her into the carrier with treats, and she whined a bit in the car. Once she was released in the motor home, she nibbled a few bites of kibble and disappeared into the bedroom again.

After the dinner dishes had been washed and put away and we were settled down with our computers, she ventured out of her hiding place, creeping warily through the hallway and scurrying back to safety at the slightest noise. She finally made it to David's chair where she demanded constant petting and reassurance.

Each day she became a little braver, jumping up on the back of the sofa or the dashboard and inspecting the new scenery she discovered outside the windows. She spent most of the nights on the bed with us, but I did find her on the floor in front of the driver's seat a morning or two. The last evening before we came home, she had become comfortable enough with her surroundings that we brought out the squirt bottle to let her know that kitchen counters and dining tables are off limits even when camping. She finally settled on the middle of the dashboard as the appropriate perch from which to survey and rule her new kingdom.

We're all back home now after a successful test run, and we're looking forward to venturing a little further soon. Kitty seems to have suffered no ill effects from her first camping adventure. Hopefully, next time she'll adjust more quickly – and hopefully, next time we'll have a working refrigerator.

Chapter 39

Kitty, Where Are You? – 11/4/18

Kitty had quite an adventure this week. It could have served as a learning experience, but whether her memory is long enough for it to make a difference remains to be seen.

When we come home, she usually meets us at the door. This is especially true if David is coming in – she recognizes the difference in the sound of our footsteps. I'm not sure if the welcome is because she misses us when we're gone or if it's because she thinks she might be able to sneak outside for a romp through the yard. Either way, it's fun to see her cute little face when we open the door, and we miss her when she's not there.

One day last week David came home while I was still at work, and not only was Kitty not at the door but the house was also very quiet. His first thought was that she had sneaked into the closet while we were getting dressed that morning and had been closed in. She wasn't there, so he called her and checked all her usual hiding places with no luck. He was beginning to worry when he heard a faint wailing and scratching that sounded like it was coming from inside the walls. He followed it until he narrowed it down to the kitchen, somewhere in the area of the stove.

The stove is against an inside wall. It has a single oven, a four-burner cook top, and a vent. Above the vent is a shallow cabinet where I store canned goods and then a square structure that encloses the exhaust pipe. The ceiling slants up toward a peak, and the space above the cabinets ranges from a few inches to almost three feet. That space is supposed to be a no-Kitty zone, but she loves to get up there when she thinks we're not looking. That day, David thought the sound was coming from that general area, but he couldn't see her. He continued to call her, and suddenly she appeared, covered with dust and looking a bit shaken.

As I said, her high perch is forbidden ground, and we reinforce that rule with a spray bottle filled with water. After her mysterious arrival, she sat huddled where she was, and she refused to move. David retrieved the spray bottle and tried to encourage her to come down. After a few squirts, she was dripping but still wouldn't budge. He realized she was scared so he stood on a chair and lifted her down. Once she was safely on the floor, he investigated.

Apparently, the hole in the top of the cabinets was cut way too big for the exhaust pipe. Since it is shielded from view by some crown molding, no one bothered to cover the opening. There are two Kitty-sized holes on either side of the pipe that lead to open spaces behind the shallow storage cabinet. Even standing on a chair I can't see the openings, but looking from the outside, I imagine they are about eight inches square and two feet deep. What I can't imagine is how Kitty managed to fit her chubby little body into the space in the first place, and then how she managed to twist around and climb back out. I can't say for sure that she has learned her lesson, but so far she hasn't been back to revisit the scene of her crime.

That's not the only traumatic experience she's had lately, but I'll save the other one for another column. I will, however, give you a hint. I'm trying to train her to wear a halter and leash so she can go outside occasionally in relative safety. I'll let you know which of us gives up first.

Chapter 40

Kitty Unchained — 11/11/18

In the last chapter I mentioned that I'm trying to train Kitty to wear a harness and walk on a leash. It's not as far-fetched as it sounds. I have a cousin whose cat loves his leash – so much, in fact, that he will stand on her chest and give her a death stare when he wants to go for "walkies." A couple of months ago I asked her if she thought it was possible to train Kitty at her advanced age. She said that with time and patience she thought it could definitely be done.

The next time we made a Walmart run, I chose an inexpensive harness in a pretty shade of blue. No bling, though. We'll wait on that until after we see how she reacts. I hesitated a bit on the size. I knew a small wouldn't work, but I was afraid a large would fall off. I finally settled on a medium, hoping she wasn't bigger than fourteen inches around the chest, and I found a leash to match. All the way home, I wondered if I had wasted my ten dollars.

The first step, according to my cousin, was to leave the harness on the floor for a week or so until Kitty was used to having it around. As soon as I got home, I removed the tags and the little plastic things that held it together. You know the ones – they have a thin thread of plastic between two tabs, and when you cut them off, you invariably lose one end and step on it later when you're barefoot. I asked David what you call them, and he said, "A pain in the rear." He's not much help. Anyway, after removing the excess packaging and adjusting it to a size I thought would fit her, I held the harness down where Kitty could sniff it. Her reaction was somewhere between minor interest and total indifference. I put it on the carpet, and she lay beside it for thirty minutes before totally ignoring it for the next week.

Next, I put the harness in the kitchen beside her food bowl. She ignored it for a few days, so one morning while I was petting her, I rubbed the buckle across her back a few times. She was so busy with her breakfast that she barely noticed, so I moved it in front of her bowl. The next morning when she approached her bowl, one foot was inside the harness and one was outside. I very carefully moved her paw into place and pulled the straps around her chest – or nearly around. The ends were two inches short of meeting. By then, she had noticed what I was doing, so she gave me a haughty look and stalked away. I let out the harness to its full extension, and put it back beside her bowl.

That weekend was clear, and we left the front door open to let some sun in through the storm door. Kitty strolled over and gazed out, watching the birds and squirrels and such. I saw an opportunity, so I laid the harness in front of the door. She gave me an in-your-dreams look and went back to one of her window perches. Not one to give up easily, I put a few treats by the harness and went about my business. It wasn't long before she was back at the door, sniffing at the treats with her feet very close to the harness. I slowly knelt beside her, moved her feet into position, and fastened the enlarged harness into place. I grabbed the leash, snapped it around her, and asked David to take a picture before we ventured outside.

David is a good photographer, but the sun was shining straight in the door, and all he could get was a black ball. While he tried several angles, Kitty realized something was different, and she lost interest in the treats. She lay down for a few seconds, and then she took off down the hall – and right out of the harness. Apparently, her feet weren't in position after all. It's hard to tell with all that fur hanging down, especially when she's in a half crouch. Anyway, I called it a day and moved the harness back to her food bowl.

This past week, she's been a bit wary, so I haven't done anything except to occasionally rub her with the harness while I'm petting her. Then, Saturday was another sunny day. When I moved the harness to the doorway, I noticed Kitty was on high alert with her ears sticking straight up, so I put it in place and went back to my computer. Later I noticed that she and David were by the door. He was encouraging her to step into the harness, and she was stepping over it and rubbing against his leg. They both tired of that game after a few rounds, so he put the harness on one of the two TV tables she frequents. She spent some time stretched out on the tables, but she made sure to be on the end as far away from the harness as possible.

My cousin assures me that once Kitty comes to associate the harness with going outside, she'll let me put it on her without a fight. We'll see if I have enough time and patience left to keep trying until that happens.

Chapter 41

Kitty's Second Christmas – 12/2/18

Kitty came to live with us in June of 2015, and a lot has changed since that mouthy little fur ball walked out from under our porch and into our hearts. She has become a big part of our lives, and she has become one of the favorite subjects for my columns, both for me as the writer and for my readers as well. I met another reader this weekend who recognized me. At least she knew my name, but she still identified me strongly with Kitty. That's okay with me. She's usually the more interesting of the two of us anyway.

Sunday afternoon I was going through some old files in my computer, looking for inspiration. I came across one of those nuggets writers love to find – an unfinished project that, even though it was abandoned for some reason, seems to have potential now. What I found was a paragraph I wrote about Kitty's second Christmas with us.

Since David and I moved to Emory, we haven't made a big deal out of Christmas. For one thing, our Christmas decorations are in the very back of the loft in our storage shed. Even if they haven't devolved into one huge rats' nest, it would take a lot work to dig them out. In addition, we live in a single-wide mobile home that has lots of windows, very little available wall space, and no space for storing furniture that would have to be moved to make room for a tree. We also don't have room for overnight guests, so we're rarely home for Christmas. And then there's Kitty.

In spite of our best efforts to avoid having a house cat, when the weather turned wet and cold, she wormed her way into the utility room. From there, it was only the thickness of a door between her and the rest of the house. By the time Christmas of 2015 rolled around, we knew we had to limit decorations or accept the fact that we'd be picking up stray pieces of tinsel and wayward ornaments for several weeks. The next year, we gave up any pretense of decorating and just enjoyed the festive homes of friends and the décor of public places we visited. This brings me to Kitty's second Christmas in 2016 and to the discarded paragraph I found:

###

We've cut way down on the gift-giving. Neither of us is big on shopping, and space limitations have required a rule of "nothing new comes in unless something old goes out." Still, we do exchange a few small gifts on Christmas morning. I didn't want Kitty to feel left out, so I bought her a few new toys. I removed them from their original packaging and put them into a plastic bag, wondering if she'd be interested but expecting her to ignore everything except the tissue paper from our gifts. I put the bag on the floor between our packages and went into the bathroom to brush my teeth. By the time I went back to the living room, she was prancing around with a gold lamé fish in her mouth. While David and I were opening our gifts, I looked down and saw only her back legs and tail sticking out of the bag. By the time we finished, all her new toys were spread throughout the living room. Nothing lifts the Christmas spirit like successful gift-giving.

###

That was two years ago, and Christmas is here again. I promised Santa in my letter that I'd take care of David and Kitty, so I'd better get busy. None of us really needs anything, but maybe I can come up with a few things that will bring a smile or a flick of the tail. And if I get really creative, maybe Christmas 2018 will be worth a column or two.

Chapter 42

Kitty and the Blanket War – 1/13/19

One of my favorite Christmas presents this year was a blanket or, more accurately, a throw. The love seat where I usually sit in the living room is in one of the colder spots in the house, and I always have an afghan or other cover within reach in case of a sudden chill. Kitty has a fondness for warm covers, but she generally prefers them to be neatly folded and on the end of the couch where David sits – until now, that is.

The new throw was given to me by Pastor Jason, my soon-to-be ex-boss, and his wife Stacy. They said I might need it to keep me warm while I spend my free time after retiring either reading or writing a book. It's microfiber with a soft plush finish on one side and a woolly look on the other, and it's very warm.

Kitty didn't pay any attention to it at first, so I had it all to myself until one night last week. I couldn't sleep, so I went into the living room to read. Kitty followed me and made the rounds of her usual roosting spots, looking out the windows into the darkened yard to be sure there were no intruders. Satisfied that her kingdom was safe, she came over to see what I was doing. She sniffed my book and rubbed her whiskers against the edges until she lost interest. Then, she discovered the blanket.

The throw is fairly wide, and the excess was spread on the seat beside me. Kitty had been standing on my legs, and when she decided to move to the empty spot, she reached out a tentative paw to test the unfamiliar surface. She patted it with one foot, and then stepped down with both feet – and she began to purr, something she rarely does. She lay down, closed her eyes and began to knead the blanket. She was soon fast asleep, and she stayed there until my eyes grew tired and I went back to bed.

It was nice having her on my side of the living room instead of with David, so the next night I enticed her with the blanket. It worked, and she spent a good bit of the evening with me. Then, Saturday afternoon during the football games, the balance of power shifted. The house was warmer, and the blanket was lying in a pile beside me, wooly side up. Before I realized what was happening, Kitty was snuggled into her newfound nest with a look of triumph on her face. I took a picture of her and posted it on Facebook, and here are some of the comments:

> **Candis**: She has attitude in those eyes!
> **Linda**: Yes she does. I think she was saying "Would you be still and get that camera out of my face!"
> **Tim**: SERIOUS attitude! The look of a Queen, not wanting to be disturbed!
> **Candis**: I'm thinking that's Kitty's blanket, not yours.
> **Linda**: Yep!
> **Candis**: It's a good thing you know when to surrender.
> **Note**: That picture is on the cover of this book.
> I enjoyed the friendly banter with my friends, but I didn't

take it too seriously until Sunday afternoon. We were watching football again, and I was working on my columns for the paper, but Kitty had her own agenda. She is usually very polite and jumps over me or walks around; Sunday she walked right across my keyboard. A moment later she returned by the same route, and she continued her periodic treks for the next few minutes until I finally realized what she wanted.

I had the throw wrapped around my legs, and there was no excess for her bed. I untucked an edge and spread it out for her, and she lay down for a few minutes. It still wasn't what she wanted, though, and she was still restless. I gave up and gave her the blanket, wooly side up. I was too warm anyway.

All is not lost in the blanket war. By Sunday evening, Kitty had lost interest in the novel surfaces and had returned to her customary perches. As I write this, she is resting on the back of the loveseat behind my head, and I am warmly wrapped up. I'm not sure if this is a temporary truce or a permanent peace, but the experience has reconfirmed in both our minds who is really in charge in this relationship.

116

Chapter 43

Kitty's Back! – 2/10/19

Kitty has been in a strange mood for the last several weeks. I know you're thinking *How could you tell?* – and that's a valid question. Let's just say her behavior has been a different kind of strange.

I'm not sure what put her into her latest tail spin, but I have a couple of ideas. A week or so ago, we were getting ready for bed, and I heard an unfamiliar noise coming from the kitchen.

"That sounded like Kitty jumping on top of the cabinets," I said to David. He agreed, so I went to the kitchen to investigate. Sure enough, there she was, staring down at me from the cabinet above the refrigerator. I retrieved the squirt bottle and proceeded to try and convince her of the error of her ways. By the time she made it back to the floor, she was pretty wet, and I didn't see much of her for the next few days.

She also had a small run-in with David over whether or not she was going out the back door in front of him. She's pretty quick, but his legs are longer, so he managed to grab her before she got away. He ended up with several scratches on his hands, but she ended up back in the house, so after that she was mad at both of us. She spent most of her time for several days in the bedroom on top of the laundry hamper or the cedar chest.

I really believe, though, that the main cause of her ill humor was the stray cats that have been hanging around the house this week – lots of stray cats. I don't know what the sudden attraction was, but we've seen several strays in the yard. One morning three of them were lined up on the ground in front of the dining room window, staring in as if to say *Can Kitty come out and play?* One of them even came up on the back porch to issue a personal invitation, but Kitty was not impressed with the invasion of her territory.

One morning we had thunder storms, and a cat who was afraid of the noise hid out on the front porch for a while, wailing loudly. Kitty spent the next two days patrolling from one window to another, making sure her house was safe from intruders.

I haven't seen any extra cats in the last several days, and Saturday, Kitty seemed to emerge from her self-imposed solitary confinement. She had been making a quick appearance each night to get her bedtime snack, but Saturday, she hung around in the bathroom while I brushed my teeth and acted halfway friendly when I doled out her treats.

In the wee hours of Sunday morning, I woke up to find her sitting with her weight equally distributed between the headboard, my pillow, and my face. I wasn't thrilled with her seating choice, but at least she wasn't ignoring me. I moved around until she went in search of a more comfortable perch, but later in the morning, she came back and snuggled up against my stomach.

Of course, it could be the colder weather that has drawn her back to us. Sunday afternoon I wasn't using "her" blanket, and she spent the afternoon napping on it with her paws resting on my arm. She didn't want David to feel left out, so she spent a little time with him on the couch, too.

So it would seem that Kitty is back to her normal place in the family – at least until the next time something upsets her little feline applecart. It's frustrating at times, but without her I'd have much less to write about.

Chapter 44

The Good Light – 3/10/19

I've learned a lot about good and bad light from Connie, my photographer neighbor. Good light results in pictures that make me look like I want to look, and bad light makes me look like I do in a changing room mirror under the awful lighting the retail stores seem to favor.

It's difficult to take good pictures inside our home, at least in the daytime. There are windows in every room, and I've learned that natural light pouring in from one of those windows results in washed out photos and lots of silhouettes. After several unsuccessful attempts to capture Kitty in her condo, which is in front of a large window, Connie advised me to change my position by ninety degrees so the light would illuminate my subject from the side. The result is one of my favorite pictures of Kitty. She is looking out through one of the round holes in the side of the condo with a regal look on her face and a halo of light bouncing off her shiny fur. You can see it on the front cover.

Connie knows I hate having my picture taken, so she gives me tips on how to pose to achieve better results. Her tips include lift your chin, lean into the camera, relax your shoulders, and in a group shot, don't put your arms around those on either side of you – it adds pounds!

Last year, a friend gave me a purple suede jacket she no longer wore, and I wrote an article about it. Ever since she read that article, Connie has wanted me to model the jacket for her, but I've never gotten around to it. Earlier this year I wore it to church, and when we got home, I asked David to take a picture of me that I could send to Connie. He was just unlocking the door, so he turned and took a quick shot of me with his phone. When I sent it to Connie, she fussed at David for not giving me time to pose, but she said the lighting was good. Apparently, the flat light of a cloudy day makes for good pictures. I had worn a pink top and purple accessories with the jacket, and the look brought out Connie's creative side. If you see a photo shoot happening at Heritage Park on a cloudy day, you'll know she's working on some new photos for my writing endeavors.

This past Sunday, I had an experience that enlarged my understanding of good light. Before the morning service, I was visiting with a friend when she said something to someone behind me, and I turned and saw a camera pointed in our direction. Stacy, our pastor's wife, has been taking pictures lately to be used on the new website that is in development. We protested briefly, but she replied, "No, no! You're in a good light!"

After I sat down, I wondered if I had followed Connie's posing advice, but as time for the service drew near, my mind turned to more serious subjects. The sermon series for February was "The Marks of a True Disciple," and there was a lot of emphasis on light. One verse in particular stuck in my mind.

> *But if we walk in the Light as He Himself is in the Light, we have fellowship with one another, and the blood of Jesus His Son cleanses us from all sin. 1 John 1:7*

That's what I call really good light.

Chapter 45

Kitty Keeps Us Straight – 3/17/19

When I say that Kitty keeps us straight, I don't mean that she keeps us on the straight and narrow. What I mean is that, because she is a curious cat, and she always wants to be where she's not, we have learned to put things away and batten down the hatches.

Like most cats, Kitty enjoys batting small objects around the floor before knocking them under the grandfather clock or between the refrigerator and cabinet. Then, she stares mournfully after the lost toy until I put my laptop aside and retrieve the toy. She thanks me by either knocking it back into hiding or marching away with her nose and tail in the air.

She's particular about the small objects, mostly ignoring the toys from the pet store in favor of grape stems or wadded up Sweet N Low packages from the trash can. In our kitchen, there's no space for a large covered container, so we use a small, open one that's the perfect height for a snoopy cat. Her choices aren't as bad as they could be, but I don't really enjoy leaning over to pick them up – or retrieving them from under the clock. The grape stems are a pain, though, if she decides to chew them up and leave little pieces all over the place. We've learned to push the favored items down under a larger one in the can and to empty the trash frequently.

We've also learned not to leave small objects on top of the bathroom countertops. Favorites are tubes of lip balm, plastic dose cups from cold medicines, caps from any kind of tube, safety pins, and anything else that moves easily and makes noise on the tile floor.

In addition to small items, Kitty loves doors – any size or shape, going in or out. As long as it's open, she wants to go through it. We've learned that, if she's missing, the first place to look is the closet. No matter how carefully I watch, she manages to slip in unnoticed. Sometimes she signals that she's been shut in by waving her paw under the door, or sometimes she sits patiently waiting for it to open. Mostly, though, she curls up on the extra blankets in the corner and takes a nap. After closing her in a few times, we've become pretty good at checking when we're finished. If she's taken up residence, instead of trying to coax her out, we leave the door ajar and yell to anyone within hearing distance, "Kitty's in the closet." That way, when one or the other of us sees her strolling through the living room later, we can run into the bedroom and close the door. It's about the only exercise we get these days – that and picking up grape stems.

Two other doors that fascinate her are the office door and the door to the small bathroom in the front of the house. David doesn't like her to come into the office, mostly because he's afraid she'll disrupt his filing system which consists of stacks of papers on various surfaces including the floor. He knows what's in each stack, but after Kitty has taken a stroll through them, no one knows.

The bathroom door fascinates her, well, mainly because it's closed, but also because there is a shower curtain which makes the tub a perfect Kitty hiding place. Besides that, there are two potted Peace Lilies in there. One was a Christmas gift from a special friend, and the other was sent to Mom's funeral, so they have sentimental value. But to Kitty, they're just a nice salad with a side of dirt. That's why they ended up in the bathroom. I always close the door, but David sometimes forgets. A couple of weeks ago, he was in there, and I heard a thump.

"Kitty knocked over one of the plants," called David.

I looked up in time to see him heading down the hall, probably to get a broom. He had apparently set the pot back up, but he had left the door open, and Kitty was up on her hind legs, elbow deep in potting soil.

"Door...open...Kitty," I spluttered as I set my laptop aside and rose from the love seat.

Kitty doesn't pay much attention to me when I speak, but when I get up, she knows I mean business. She was out of the bathroom and at the other end of the house before I could get the words lined up in my mouth.

I'd like to say that David always closes the door now, but that would only be true about half the time. Still, the plants are doing well and haven't suffered any more attacks. I'm planning to move them out on our new front porch when the weather warms up enough. There won't be any small, toy-like objects anywhere in the vicinity, and there won't be any closet doors to attract undue attention. I'm hoping the neighborhood strays won't discover the porch or the plants and think I've installed a new feline salad bar.

124

Chapter 46

Pets and Their Rituals — 6/2/19

Kitty came to live with us four years ago this month. Although her assimilation into our family has not always been smooth, we've worked out routines that work for all of us. Some of them have even become rituals.

Kitty makes no secret of the fact that David is her favorite, but since I'm the first one up after a long, lonely night, she's usually glad to see me. When I come into the kitchen, she stands by her feeding station and looks at me pitifully. While I scoop kibble into her bowl, she runs around the island counter clockwise, stops in front of her bowl, and looks up again. This time she has a more demanding look, asking without words why I'm not petting her.

In the beginning, any time I touched her became "bite and scratch" play time, so now when she wants me to pet her, I obediently comply. She sometimes wants to be scratched, and she walks around making sure I hit just the right spots. Occasionally, she even pushes her head against my hand so I can scratch behind her ears. When hunger gets the best of her, she begins to nibble her food and finally crouches down and begins to eat seriously. When she's had all the petting she wants, she makes a pretend lunge at my hand to let me know I'm free to go about my own morning routine.

David's morning usually includes some time at his laptop which is set up on one side of the dining table. When Kitty sees him heading in that direction, she jumps into his chair and waits expectantly. He bumps her gently with his hand and tells her to move over. If she doesn't comply immediately, he sits on the edge of the chair and scoots over slowly until she jumps to the chair beside him. Then she proceeds to bump his elbow with her head until he pets her. When she's had enough petting, she settles down for a nap, and he gets on with his morning.

She sleeps most of the day, but she varies her napping spots, maybe to throw off any predators who might slip into the house. Her most obvious places are her cat condo, the sofa, or our bed – either on it or under it. She has other places we have yet to discover where she disappears from time to time, just to keep us on our toes. But in the evening, she reverts to being more predictable.

Her favorite toy of the moment is a stuffed fish attached to a stick with an elastic string. Once we've settled down in front of the TV after dinner, we hear the sound of the stick being dragged across the ceramic tile in the kitchen and we know she's bringing her fish from the bedroom to drop at David's feet. Then she ignores the fish and jumps up onto the couch and lies down for another nap, either very close to him or at the other end. Later, when he settles down in bed to read for a bit before turning out the light, we hear the stick on the tile again, and she deposits the fish between his feet.

Her final ritual of the day, another food related event, is her bedtime treats. I've explained that ritual several times, so I won't go through the whole routine. Suffice it to say that as soon as the last treat is gone, she jumps off the bed and disappears until morning when the rituals begin again.

We're house and dog sitting this week, and I was surprised to find that Kitty is not the only animal that likes rituals. It seems that Spike has developed a routine of his own. When it came time to feed him the first night, I was surprised to find his bowl in the tub in the garage where the food is kept. In addition, there was a rather comfy-looking chair next to it. Just to see what happened, I put food in the bowl and placed it on the floor by the food tub instead of on the patio where I've fed him in the past. I called Spike, and he ambled in like he knew what to expect. He didn't begin eating immediately but stood giving me a look that resembled the one Kitty gives me in the mornings.

"Do you want some petting?" I asked, and based on his reaction, he did. He still didn't eat, so I asked if I was supposed to sit in the chair. Again, his actions indicated that I was right.

It seems that pets, like people, find comfort in rituals. It makes me wonder how Kitty gets along when we leave her for several days at a time. Maybe that's why she's so mad at us when we get home.

Chapter 47

Kitty Meets a Fan — 7/28/19

Kitty is not a celebrity who seeks the spotlight. She is more like Greta Garbo, the Swedish-American movie star of the 1920's and 30's who is famous for the line, *I want to be alone*. Unlike some family pets who never meet a stranger, Kitty hides under the bed when visitors come, and even though she tries to sneak outside occasionally, she seems to prefer watching life go by from behind a pane of glass. However, the rules and regulations of society don't favor the sensitivities of the recluse, and this week she had to go out into the world.

When she makes it outside, Kitty seems to be a prime target for fleas and other insects that make a furry feline itch. Even when she stays indoors, the pests seem to make it inside, possibly hitching a ride on jeans or shoes. Regardless of how they get there, Kitty is very aware of their presence, and so are we when she chooses to scratch in the middle of the bed at 3:00 am or when she evicts the little varmints into the couch or the carpet.

Thankfully, veterinary science has found a solution. Flea protection has progressed from the old-fashioned flea collar to a small tube of liquid that, when applied four times a year, ensures a scratch-free environment. This convenient remedy comes at a cost, though.

First, it's quite expensive, but pet owners spare no expense when it comes to their fur babies. Second, it's not easy to apply, at least on Kitty. The instructions say to part the hair and apply the solution directly to the skin. Good luck with that when the subject cat has extremely thick fur and won't sit still long enough for their people to reach the skin. And third, the flea protection is only available by prescription, and the law requires the vet to see the patient at least once a year.

David mentioned recently that it was time to renew Kitty's defense, so last week we dropped by the vet's office. Apparently it had been over a year since she had visited this particular clinic because David came back empty handed. Kitty had her annual shots at the Sulphur Springs clinic, but they don't dispense this type of flea medicine. So we went home and began the ordeal of transporting Kitty.

David retrieved the pet carrier from the shed and set it on the floor with the door open. Cats are naturally curious, so she will sometimes walk in on her own. Not this time. He tried to tempt her with treats, but she saw right through him and ran off. He threw up his hands in defeat, so I went to the refrigerator for some milk. She always comes running for milk. However, before I opened the carton, she reappeared and walked into the carrier. A girl just likes to do things on her own schedule sometimes.

We made it to the vet's office with no further problems and were ushered immediately into an examining room. David set Kitty's carrier on the floor, and we waited a long while - at least it seemed long to Kitty who was trapped in a box. She pressed her face against the air holes on the side close to me and let out a plaintive meow. She's a lady of few words, but when she speaks, she's very expressive.

I squatted down and put two fingers through the mesh, expecting her to express her feelings with teeth and claws. Instead, she pushed her face against my fingers and let me do the unthinkable - scratch under her chin. After being sufficiently reassured, she retired to the towel she had wadded up in the back. When the vet finally came in, I thought we were going to have to tip the carrier and pour her out, but her curiosity again got the better of her, and she came out on her own.

The examination was superficial - taking her weight and temperature. She continued to behave well, and we were soon on our way. I stopped at the reception desk to pay, and David set Kitty down in the lobby to take advantage of another minute or two of air conditioning.

While I fished for my credit card, I heard a voice say, "Is that Kitty?" One of the ladies from my book club - and a City Girl reader - was standing at the lobby counter.

"Yes," I answered. "That's her." We chatted until my credit card receipt was ready. I could see her out of the corner of my eye as she leaned down and talked to Kitty. On Saturday, we sat next to each other at the book club meeting, and I asked how Kitty had reacted to her visit.

"Oh, she was just like you describe her," she answered. "She came closer to the door of the cage, but not too close, and she stared at me as if to say, 'Who are you and why are you looking at me?'"

Apparently Kitty wasn't impressed at being approached by a fan. In fact, she wasn't impressed with the whole afternoon. Back at home she wanted nothing to do with having flea medication applied to the back of her neck, and she couldn't decide whether she wanted anything to do with us. She alternated between rubbing against our ankles for attention and jumping out from a hiding place and biting those same ankles. I guess that kind of temperamental behavior is to be expected from a star who has spent her day dealing with her adoring public.

Chapter 48

Kitty Welcomes Us Home — 8/25/19

David and I made a quick trip to Louisiana for some family business last week. We left Thursday morning and returned Saturday afternoon. If we're going to be gone for a week or so, we line up someone to come in and check on Kitty, but for a couple of days, Kitty does fine on her own. All she needs is a liter and a half of water in her gravity waterer, half a dozen scoops of food in her large food bowl, and a clean litter box, and she's good to go.

I think she probably slept most of the time we were gone because I didn't see anything broken or even out of place, but she was glad to see us. She ran back and forth between us for petting until David went across the street for coffee with Charles. After that, she settled down in her condo for a nap. She did visit me long enough to rub her chin on the edge of my computer table and let me scratch between her eyes for a couple of seconds. But when she nipped at me, I withdrew my hand, and she went back to her nap.

When David got back, we had a snack supper, both because I didn't have anything thawed and because we wanted to watch the Cowboys/Texans game while we ate. We borrowed the two TV tables that have become one of Kitty's favorite perches. I don't know if it was because we took her tables or because the excitement of having us home had worn off and she remembered that she was mad at us for leaving her. Either way, she copped an attitude and began to harass David.

During dinner she flipped his letter opener off the coffee table, and then, she went after his glasses. She stood on her hind legs and tried to pull the bowl of grapes off his TV table. When dinner was over and her TV tables were returned to their proper place, she lay down by David and immediately began to scratch the sofa cushions.

All these actions earned her a squirt from the water bottle, but I'm not sure how effective that is as a deterrent these days. When Kitty does something wrong and David reaches for the bottle, she turns her head toward him and squeezes her eyes shut as if daring him to squirt her. I think it's become a game with her.

She finally tired of the game and settled down on the carpet at David's feet for another nap. At one point, I asked where she was and David pointed her out. She must have heard her name, because she woke up long enough to earn another squirt of water for scratching the side of the couch.

We didn't hear much more from her until bedtime. I stayed in the living room for a little while after David went into the bathroom to wash his face and brush his teeth. She frantically ran back and forth between us, trying to make sure one or the other of us didn't sneak out without her knowing it. When I finally went into the bedroom, she continued to run laps from the bedroom to the kitchen, probably to make sure I didn't forget her bedtime snacks.

By Sunday morning, she had pretty much settled back into her normal routine. She occasionally ran over to one of us to stand possessively on a foot and allow us to pet her for a moment before returning to more urgent Kitty business. She seems to miss us more when we're gone than she did when she was younger. We may have to arrange for her to have visitors when we travel in the future. We could, of course, take her with us. That should provide lots of writing material.

A NOTE FROM KITTY
AS TOLD TO HER BIOGRAPHER

So that's the first four years of Kitty's Story. As she's become more mature, the chaos around the Brendle home has diminished – but so has the writing material. When people greet me now with "How's Kitty?" my usual reply is "Fat and sassy" instead of some cute story that would make a good column. I'm sure she will continue to cause an occasional commotion, but only time will tell whether her actions will lead to another book. Regardless, she appreciates your love and adoration, and she hopes you enjoyed her story.

Blessings and purrs,

Linda & Kitty

ABOUT THE AUTHOR

Linda Brendle first began to write during her years as a caregiver. After two memoirs about Alzheimer's caregiving, **A Long and Winding Road** *and* **Mom's Long Good-Bye**, she ventured into the world of fiction. She has published two novels, **Tatia's Tattoo** and **Fallen Angel Salvage**, and is currently working on **Salvaged**, a third novel about Tatia.

Linda is retired from the business world, but she still holds an on-line position as the Financial Manager for Square Core Media. She also blogs and writes a column for the weekly newspaper in the tiny East Texas town where she and her husband David live and take care of the needs and wants of their once feral cat Kitty.

Photo courtesy of Constance Ashley, Photographer, www.constanceashley.com.

MORE BOOKS BY LINDA BRENDLE

A Long and Winding Road: A Caregiver's Tale of Life, Love, and Chaos: This memoir is the story of the hilarity and chaos that happen when four people, two of whom have Alzheimer's, spend seven weeks traveling through sixteen states in a forty-foot motor home. It is also the story of the lives and experiences that led these four people to this particular place and time in their lives.

Mom's Long Goodbye: A Caregiver's Tale of Alzheimer's, Grief, and Comfort: After finishing **Winding Road**, many readers asked what happened next. Mom's Long Goodbye is the rest of the story. Mom's goodbye began with a red photo album and ended fifteen years later in a hospital bed in the Alzheimer's wing of Southridge Village. This is her story and mine.

Tatia's Tattoo: As a successful D.C. lawyer, Tatia's mission in life is to destroy the sex trafficking trade in small-town America. She knows where to find it. She's been there. Filled with tragedy, crime, redemption, and love, **Tatia's Tattoo** is a story that exposes the sordid underbelly of small towns and shines a light of hope on how the evil might be defeated.

Fallen Angel Salvage (Tatia's Story, Book #2): Tatia and Jesse have a perfect life in Chicago. Her testimony put Eric in prison in Texas twenty years ago. How could anything go wrong? An old black van. A missing child. Tatia and Jesse race through the city streets with a band of bikers while Johnny and Jade dig through the dark web and Detectives Nelson and Martin pound on doors. Will it be enough? Or will their daughter become another statistic?

CPSIA information can be obtained
at www.ICGtesting.com
Printed in the USA
LVHW081154080821
694360LV00008B/96

9 781734 210804